IF RUSSIA WINS

Carlo Masala is Professor of International Politics at the Bundeswehr University Munich. He previously worked as Deputy Director in the research department at the NATO Defence College in Rome. Since January 2024, Masala has been Director of the Centre for Intelligence and Security Studies at the University of the Federal Armed Forces in Munich. He received the Lichtenberg Medal in Gold from the Lower Saxony Academy of Sciences in Göttingen in 2023 for his academic work and science communication. *If Russia Wins* was an immediate #1 bestseller upon publication in Germany and has since become a bestseller in the Netherlands.

IF RUSSIA WINS

A Scenario

CARLO MASALA

Translated from the German by
Olena Ebel and Ruth Ahmedzai Kemp

Atlantic Books
London

Originally published in Germany as *Wenn Russland Gewinnt* in 2025
by Verlag C. H. Beck, Munich.

First published in paperback in Great Britain in 2025 by Atlantic Books,
an imprint of Atlantic Books Ltd.

10 9 8 7 6

A CIP catalogue record for this book is available from the British Library.

Paperback ISBN: 978 1 80546 574 4
E-book ISBN: 978 1 80546 575 1

Printed and bound by CPI (UK) Ltd, Croydon CR0 4YY

Atlantic Books
An imprint of Atlantic Books Ltd
Ormond House
26–27 Boswell Street
London
WC1N 3JZ

www.atlantic-books.co.uk

Product safety EU representative: Authorised Rep Compliance Ltd., Ground Floor, 71 Lower Baggot Street, Dublin, D02 P593, Ireland. www.arccompliance.com

Contents

IF RUSSIA WINS

Introduction

The heroine is under pressure. The villain has her in a stranglehold, her gun is out of reach, the plane full of explosives is heading straight for the White House. The audience holds its breath. The situation seems hopeless. But then comes the twist! She wriggles out of his grip, grabs the gun, steers the plane upwards – and after the close call comes the happy ending.

We are used to thinking that everything will be fine. That is how it works in every Hollywood film. That is how it was in 1945 and 1989. Not straight away – that would be boring. But eventually, everything turns out okay. Sure, our democracy, Ukraine and the West are under pressure. Populists are winning elections, Russian troops are advancing, Donald Trump is president. But in the end, it won't be so bad. Russia won't attack us, our democracy will survive, the West will remain strong.

But what if things don't turn out that way? What if Russia wins?

To understand what is at stake and which decisions could have which consequences, we need to know what could happen. This is the strength of thinking through scenarios. In science, but also in political and military planning, scenario-based strategizing is a method of simulating future developments based on current trends and events. The aim is to identify the conditions and factors that might determine these developments and to extrapolate creatively from the present.

Scenarios expand the realm of possibilities in our minds. They serve to counteract intellectual complacency and short-term political horizons. What is at stake in Ukraine and in our time only really sinks in when we think about what could happen if things do not turn out well.

It is possible that Russia will win in Ukraine. Perhaps it will even have won by the time this book is published – who can say for sure? Although, it seems to me it's already a Russian victory if they manage to keep the territory they have occupied. Now, some people may not care about Ukraine. And quite a few may think, 'It will be good if the war finally ends. Then things can go back to normal. Just give Russia what it wants, then there will be peace.' But is that so? Is it really just about Ukraine? What if this is only the beginning? What if European security and our entire liberal world order are at stake, and we are once again sticking our heads in the sand? The scenario I present in this book explores how all this could play out.

INTRODUCTION

The future is always open. No one knows what it holds, and no one can foresee all the factors and interactions that will determine it. A scenario is therefore only one of many possible ways in which things might develop. It is important to keep this in mind when reading this book. My goal is not to prophesy. My goal is to encourage reflection, discussion and further thought. And I would also stress: we rehearse scenarios like this in order to avoid them happening in real life.

My scenario is based on data, academic research, and discussions I have had over the past two years with many colleagues – as well as experts within government and the armed forces whose job it is to consider the implications of a Russian victory in Ukraine on developing security policy. I have also incorporated insights from tabletop exercises where I was able to participate either actively or as an observer. However, this scenario, in the form presented here, has been developed by me alone. In security and defence policy circles, other scenarios have been played out and discussed, including a comprehensive military operation against a NATO member state. Mine is not presented in an academic or scholarly format, although it has been developed according to academic standards. In addition to a purely descriptive account of events, I've included imagined dialogues, allowing readers to feel like they are observing the action from up close. Finally, this scenario is highly condensed. In reality, the way things unfolded would be much more complex. Countless discussions and meetings would take place at the operational level, and there would certainly be hundreds of phone calls and video conferences between the parties involved. For the sake of readability, I have omitted much of this detail and focused on the major events.

I have had the opportunity to talk to many people in the course of writing this book, and I would like to extend my thanks to them all. I would especially like to thank Sebastian Ullrich at my German publisher C. H. Beck, who supported the creation of this book in his usual calm and professional manner from the very beginning, guiding the process to its conclusion as an intellectual sparring partner and brilliant editor. I would also like to thank my colleague Martin Schulze Wessel, to whom I'm grateful for the analogy of the remilitarization of the Rhineland.

Carlo Masala, August 2025

Narva, Estonia

27 March 2028

The city wakes up to explosions in the early hours of the morning. Two Russian brigades invade Narva from the north and the east. The masked attackers quickly overpower the Estonian border troops. The Russian soldiers also encounter little resistance in Narva itself, and what they do encounter they're quick to shatter. They have support among parts of the local civil population, who have been supplied with small arms and machine guns in the previous weeks and months. Located in the border area with Russia, this is Estonia's third-largest city, with a population of 57,000. It is conquered within a matter of hours. By sunrise, the Russian flag is flying from the tower of the historic city hall. Video clips of the hoisting of the flag are circulating across social media in near real time, with the hashtag #DayOfReturn.

The Russian invasion comes out of the blue. It's true that Narva's Russian-speaking population has been demonstrating for weeks, on the grounds they're being prevented from using their language in the public sphere and from practising their culture. Spurred on by disinformation on social media, they also fear that the government in Tallinn could make them second-class citizens and deny them the right to vote. According to information spreading on Facebook and Telegram, this is because they are considered a security risk due to their closeness and ties to Russia. There have also been multiple skirmishes between these 'Russians' and the Estonian police. But all this has happened before, and the Estonian government assumed the situation would – as before – be brought under control. The massing of smaller Russian units on the border was noted but was not considered a serious threat. After all, there are NATO troops present in the country: 1,700 soldiers as part of the Enhanced Forward Presence (eFP), and 600 US infantry personnel in Võru. Policymakers have continually reassured themselves that this will provide sufficient deterrence.

Furthermore, in the days leading up to the attack, Estonia's and NATO's attention was focused on the southern part of the Estonia–Russia border, where a Russian army division has been rehearsing various manoeuvres as part of their Operation Motherland exercises. And that's how the surprise attack succeeds. A response from the British-led NATO troops stationed some 145 kilometres from Narva is out of the question within such a short time frame.

The Narva attack isn't the Russian army's only operation that night. Russian soldiers disguised as tourists have been taking ferries to the island of Hiiumaa, off the coast of Estonia, for the past few days. Now, they spring into action. They are supported by two amphibious warships from Russia's Baltic Fleet, which have made an unexpected change of course en route from St Petersburg to the international waters of the Baltic Sea, approaching Estonia's second-largest (but sparsely populated) island from the north. It is still dark when they lower their landing boats into the water, and about 400 Russian marines land off the coast of Hiiumaa to support the troops already on the island. Here, too, resistance quickly collapses. By morning, the Russian flag flies in the town of Kärdla on Hiiumaa, a town with a population of 4,000.

In just one night, Russia has seized two Estonian cities and taken the whole of NATO by surprise. Both operations make strategic sense from a Russian perspective. With Narva, they have conquered a city whose population is 88 per cent Russian-speaking; Hiiumaa offers the Russian navy the ability to threaten and, if necessary, to implement a naval blockade of the Baltic states between the Russian ports of St Petersburg in the north and Kaliningrad in the south.

One more noteworthy event from this night: the president of Belarus, Lukashenko, announces that, in the coming days, he will be sending several brigades of his country's armed forces to Astravyets, a small border town just 50 kilometres away from Vilnius, for exercises.

The attack on the Baltic states has begun.

Palais des Nations, Geneva

Three years earlier

The mood is frosty as the delegations from Ukraine and the Russian Federation meet in Geneva at the Palais des Nations. There are five representatives from each side, and they have been working on the text of the treaty for weeks, mediated by the US and China. These men and women have been at war since 2022, and it clearly shows in their faces and postures. They have all aged, even though some are barely older than thirty. The Ukrainians know what they need to do – what the US and China, but also Russia, expect from them. They have come to Geneva to sign their capitulation. It is not a formal capitulation, but the surrender of over 20 per cent of Ukrainian territory – land for which they have been fighting for years with considerable losses. But now they have neither the manpower or materiel nor the support from the West to continue the fight.

President Zelensky held a final meeting with his Western partners only the evening before. He pointed out the catastrophic consequences of a Russian victory for European security and asked for a substantial increase in aid in order to keep fighting. But the mood had shifted. It's been far too long since there was any progress, argued the US president. What battles has Ukraine won? How much land have they recaptured recently? He can't keep justifying to the American people why so much money is being spent on military support for Ukraine. If he bought Greenland for the same amount of money, the land-to-dollar ratio would be much better. 'I don't do bad deals…'

The British prime minister tried to intervene, 'Mr President, Europe—' But he didn't get to finish. 'Europe… has to pay for its own security,' came the response. Russia has lost enough men and materiel to be easily deterred in the future. It is now time to end this war. 'If Mr Zelensky wants to keep fighting, he's welcome to. But at his own expense.' There was an awkward silence in the room. 'Zelensky must realize that it's game over,' a British newspaper quoted the French president as saying, the next morning.

The EU has not managed to ramp up the production of the military equipment necessary for Ukraine's defence to a level where a constant supply can be guaranteed. So, it cannot make up for the loss of US support. Of course, almost all of Europe's top politicians, including European Commission president Ursula von der Leyen, have been repeating over and over in recent months that if the US withdraws, Europe's hour will come. But when the moment does come, it turns out it was all just empty talk, just as it has been for the past few years since the Russian full-scale invasion. The economic situation in most European countries is so fraught that governments are hesitant to spend any more on Ukraine. Also, the fear of having to take in even more Ukrainian refugees is causing the mood to shift in many places. Politicians worry about further increases in voter support for far-right and left-wing populist parties, which are successfully targeting voters by discrediting support for Ukraine. All this has left the Ukrainian president with no choice but to begin ceasefire negotiations with Russia.

The results of the talks are presented to the international public as the Geneva Peace, but in reality it is the Geneva Capitulation. Not only must Ukraine surrender over 20 per cent of its territory, it is also forced to include a permanent neutrality clause in its constitution, which rules out joining NATO. As a form of compensation, a reconstruction programme financed by the World Bank is agreed, not only for the government-controlled parts of Ukraine, but also for the territories occupied by Russia.

To monitor the ceasefire, the United Nations will commission a peacekeeping force consisting of troops from China, European countries and various other states. Its task will be to report violations of the ceasefire agreement by either side to the United Nations Security Council. However, its mandate stops short of a credible military deterrence to prevent potential new attacks by Russia.

And thus, the largest armed conflict in Europe since World War II ends with Ukraine's defeat. While Western politicians repeatedly emphasize that the territories annexed by Russia will never be recognized as Russian under international law, and that the agreement is a temporary one ('We firmly hope that in the not too distant future, we will negotiate with Russia about the return of these territories – and of course, the rest of Ukraine enjoys the full economic, political and military support of the West!'), the Russian media are celebrating the agreement for what it is: a Russian victory. Russian talk shows are busy settling scores with the West, as per usual. Various TV anchors describe NATO's failure to back Ukraine as just the beginning of the resurgence of Russia's strength and greatness in international politics. No one, they argue, should believe that Russia will simply be content with what it has already achieved. The Russian World project to bring all Russian-speaking regions back within the Russian sphere of influence is far from over. The Baltic states, Moldova and Georgia are all still in Russia's sights.

As for the West, there are precious few voices describing Ukraine's defeat as a serious threat to the

European security order. The general mood is different. Some express it openly, others more cautiously. But you sense it everywhere: the relief that this war is now over.

Europe and the United States

A wind of change

As soon as Ukraine's capitulation is signed, there is criticism of those who were vocal advocates of military and political support for Ukraine during the war with Russia. The argument put forward mostly by populist parties, on both the right and the left, is best summarized by the words of the future French president from the Rassemblement National party (formerly Front National). During his campaign, he says, 'The warmongering countries have not only almost ruined their own economies, they have also unnecessarily prolonged this war – the end result of which could have been achieved a year and a half ago – depriving thousands, if not hundreds of thousands, of Ukrainians of the chance to be alive today.'

This tone dominates the discourse in Europe and the US, giving a boost to the populist parties in the EU that have sided with Russia since the beginning of its war of aggression. These parties make gains in regional and national elections across Europe. Alongside France, Italy's right-wing government is also steering its foreign and security policy onto a new course. While Italy was one of Ukraine's supporters during the war (albeit politically more than economically or militarily), after Ukraine's capitulation the Italians are often heard demanding that a restoration of relations with Russia at least be considered.

Foreign policy priorities are also changing in the US. Now that Russia's war against Ukraine is over, at least in its high-intensity phase, there are growing calls among Republicans and Democrats alike to leave the European post-war order up to the Europeans and to focus US efforts on the Indo-Pacific region instead. And so, it's not long before there is cross-party consensus for a reduction of US troop numbers in Europe, and their re-deployment to Asia.

Russia

A thaw in Moscow?

Vladimir Putin announces his resignation, surprising the whole world, especially the correspondent of Germany's public broadcaster ARD, who just two days ago described him as an 'eternal president' ('His grip on power is stronger than ever'). In a televised address, Putin declares Russia's victory over Ukraine 'an important historic milestone on the way to Russia's return as a great power'. Russia has shown the world that 'even the world's largest and most aggressive military alliance, NATO, is unable to defeat eternal Russia and to bring it to its knees'. Now it is time to hand over the task of completing 'Russia's historic mission' to someone else. Although he won't be retiring completely to hunt and fish, he will in future be taking a role in the background, as president of the New Russia Foundation.

Putin appoints Oleg Obmanshchikov as his successor – a forty-seven-year-old economist. Of course, Putin says, the Duma still has to approve Obmanshchikov's nomination, but he foresees no problems there, since he has already informed the leaders of the major parties represented.

International media immediately launches into extensive speculation about Putin's reasons for this step. Was he forced to resign by his inner circle due to the disastrous human and economic losses suffered by Russia in the war? Is he so sick that he is handing over the reins to someone else as a precaution? Or is this another trick of the cunning KGB man? Is he trying to present, to foreign observers and his own population, a young leader eager for reform, while behind the scenes he and the FSB, the internal security service, are pulling the strings, the same as ever?

This last theory is supported by the fact that most sanctions imposed by the EU and the US are still in force, despite the Geneva treaty. A 'fresh face' could perhaps mean that they are lifted soon. Ultimately, however, it is all just conjecture. As in the past, the press has no access to the Kremlin's inner circle and is more or less in the dark when analysing Putin's motives.

What is known about Obmanshchikov is that he comes from Russia's financial sector, and that he spent some time studying in the UK in his youth and later worked for the accountancy firm Ernst & Young in Dubai. At first glance, he is the polar opposite of Putin or Sergey Lavrov: young, charismatic and cosmopolitan.

In his first official address to the nation in the Russian Duma – which, of course, is also directed towards an international audience – Obmanshchikov upholds the annexation of the Ukrainian regions of Donetsk, Luhansk, Zaporizhzhia and Kherson, as well as Crimea, describing them as part of Russia's heartland. But he also indicates that he is willing to talk to Ukraine about normalizing relations. He doesn't say what he means by that, but he does use the same memorable formula for the future relationship between Russia and Ukraine that Willy Brandt used in his inaugural speech as federal chancellor in 1969, when he described the Federal Republic of Germany and the GDR as 'two states, one nation'.

The use of this phrase causes quite a stir in Germany. It is welcomed with particular enthusiasm by members of the country's Social Democratic Party. The faction that saw former Chancellor Olaf Scholz's support for Ukraine during Russia's war of aggression as a strategic mistake now gains the upper hand within the party as well as in the parliamentary group. It's like being transported back to the eighties, when a certain Mikhail Gorbachev became general secretary of the Communist Party and fully lived up to the hopes placed on him as a reformer of Soviet communism. Why can't the same happen with Obmanshchikov, wonder many people within the SDP and beyond.

The plans to revive arms control agreements, a surprise Russia's new president springs on the world in his first few months in office, are duly noted. Naturally, there is scepticism and mistrust. Can Obmanshchikov be taken at face value, or is he just a puppet of the secret service or the military? No one, not even the various intelligence services of European countries and the US, has an answer to these questions, and getting a personal impression – at the level of heads of state and government – is difficult, with Russia still isolated internationally.

Nevertheless, everyone is looking eagerly to Moscow, hoping for a thaw after this bleak ice age. It seems many in the West are desperate to avoid a new Cold War, with the tremendous resources it would consume.

Emissaries are discreetly sent to Moscow to get a better picture of the new man in the Kremlin. The communiqués from the diplomats who have met Obmanshchikov and his inner circle personally all say more or less the same thing: it is true that 'we can't tell for sure' who is propping Obmanshchikov up, but the man himself is a 'clever, charismatic reformer, whose desire for change is obvious when you meet him in person'.

This impression is reinforced through multiple interviews that Obmanshchikov gives to the international media. There is widespread hope that a new Gorbachev reigns in Moscow, whose goal is to bring Russia out of its dark past and lead it into a new, perhaps democratic, future.

Ukraine

After Geneva: a country in chaos

Occasional messages from human rights activists in the Donbas region trickle through to the outside world and tell a different story. No sooner has the intense fighting stopped than there are massive movements of refugees from the occupied territories. Unconfirmed sources speak of up to 1.5 million people. And Russia's new president continues the Russification policy unabated. People from Russia are being resettled in the former Ukrainian territories, and Ukrainians who refuse to recognize the legitimacy of Russian rule are sent to 're-education' camps. The wave of adoptions also continues; Ukrainian children can still be adopted by Russian couples, regardless of whether they have living biological parents in Ukraine.

Yet these ongoing atrocities receive little attention from the international public. No one really seems concerned, apart from a few very active groups founded by the Ukrainian diaspora in Europe. The prevailing mood is relief at the end of the Great War, as Ukrainians refer to it. The hope and desire for brighter prospects are just too strong.

In fact, to speak of the *end* of the Great War is not entirely true, because there are repeated skirmishes on the border between Russia-occupied territories and 'free' Ukraine between Russian and Ukrainian armed forces. These skirmishes tend to last several days and cost lives on both sides. The UN monitoring mission takes note and files a report with the United Nations headquarters in New York. But that is the end of it.

In the final phase of the war, before Ukraine's capitulation, the Ukrainian army and security services smuggled in or built up a kind of partisan army in the occupied territories. Extensive weapons stores were set up for its activities. This Free Ukrainian Army, as it calls itself, regularly carries out attacks on police stations and kills Russian officials who work in the administration of the occupied territories, through car bombs or other means. After each successful attack, the Russian police, the Russian army and various Russian security services operating in the occupied territories retaliate with increased repression of the Ukrainian civil population still living there.

The situation in the rest of Ukraine is, of course, calmer. There are no more attacks by Russian drones, cruise missiles, glide bombs or ballistic missiles.

But that does not automatically make things much better. Large parts of the country resemble a pile of rubble. Countless villages and towns were razed to the ground during the war. The energy infrastructure has been severely degraded; there is often no electricity or running water. The Ukrainian state is basically bankrupt, the money given by international donor organizations for the reconstruction of the country is nowhere near enough to carry out even the most essential infrastructure projects, and unemployment continues to rise. The catastrophic economic situation means that not only are too few people who fled during the war returning, but there are also new waves of young and well-educated Ukrainians emigrating to the EU.

At the same time, old conflicts are re-emerging in Ukraine. The oligarchs and the military against the government, the president against the mayor of Kyiv, and so on. All these conflicts were put on the back burner during the war and are now resurfacing. It is a time of settling old scores.

Ukrainian civil society is on edge. Veterans and disabled people, who depend on the state welfare system, are protesting almost daily for better financial support and medical care. There are also regular demonstrations by trade unions and other interest groups, demanding their rights loudly and sometimes violently.

The tense social, political and economic situation in the country makes it easy for the Russian secret services to recruit informants who regularly provide them with intelligence from the various ministries and the armed forces. The sums of money that the Russian authorities can pay make some Ukrainians forget that they are collaborating with – or to be more precise, working for – the state that wanted to annihilate them just a few months ago. And who can blame them, given the cataclysmic state the country is in?

The desperate economic situation in Ukraine, as well as the increasingly intense social and political conflicts, leads to an unexpected revival of political forces with an eastward orientation – that is, looking towards Moscow as the only potential for an economic recovery. With active financial and organizational support from pro-Russian oligarchs and Russian secret services, accompanied by a massive disinformation campaign, these pro-Russian political forces eventually manage to win a majority in Ukraine's parliamentary elections. President Zelensky, who has far-reaching rights under the constitution, tries to prevent this change of course and dissolve parliament. But he fails, because such a move is opposed by the international community – who fear that Ukraine could become a presidential dictatorship – as well as by large parts of Ukraine's population. The prime ministers Zelensky appoints do not last long, either, because they don't have the majority in the Rada and so they are regularly ousted by the pro-Russian parliamentary majority, through one no-confidence vote after another. To prevent the country from becoming completely ungovernable, Zelensky finally resorts to calling an early presidential election, which he loses. The 'peace agreement' has plunged Ukraine into chaos.

Brussels

Limited defence capabilities

Some in NATO are asking themselves, do we need to deter Russia? And if so, are our capabilities sufficient? Before the capitulation, while major battles were still raging in Ukraine, there was a certain awareness among European countries of the need to invest in their own deterrent capabilities. But does that still apply? Although the United States continues to urge its allies to invest more in their own defence, stressing that American troop numbers in Europe will be reduced in the foreseeable future due to America's reorientation towards Asia, the discussion in many European capitals is heading in the opposite direction.

Some say that now Russia has ended its war against Ukraine – and, more importantly, with Russia's army having suffered considerable losses in the conflict – the focus of European defence efforts should be on supporting Ukraine and less so on the continued rearmament of NATO states.

Others argue that work has been ongoing for years to close the two largest capability gaps: namely Europe's inadequate air defences, and its weaknesses in terms of conventional cruise missiles with a sufficient range to reach far into Russian territory. Stationing US Dark Eagle hypersonic missiles in Wiesbaden as part of the NATO Multidomain Task Force is thought to provide sufficient deterrence. Russia would surely not dare launch a full-scale attack against a NATO member state – because, in response, important Russian airfields, military units, and logistical and communication centres could be destroyed very quickly. And the development of proprietary European systems, agreed upon by France, Poland, Italy and Germany, is well under way.

Furthermore, NATO stands head and shoulders above the Russian army in terms of conventional arms, say the harshest critics of a stronger and thus costlier defence policy. And besides, the new Russian president should be given a chance to credibly demonstrate his new moderate course. An increased build-up of arms in the West would only make it unnecessarily difficult for him to push through domestic reforms in Russia. Scaling up the deterrence policy would only achieve one thing: it would bolster conservative forces in Russia. Surely even the most trigger-happy cowboy sees this. After all, we can't ignore history. If Europe has learned one thing from the devastating wars of the twentieth century, it's that every possible means should be taken to secure peace and to break the logic of military escalation that only ever leads to destruction. There is nothing wrong with self-denial if it helps reach an understanding.

This attitude is viewed with concern in Central and Eastern Europe as well as in the Baltic states. The growing shift away from the consensus that existed during the war – that Russia poses the greatest security threat for the European continent in the foreseeable future – prompts the fear that the credibility of collective defence within the framework of NATO's Article 5 could be undermined.

Reports from the NATO military and strategic headquarters in Brussels that the alliance lacks the decisive capabilities in many areas to quickly and decisively repel a potential Russian attack on NATO territory are dismissed by most Western European governments as exaggerated. For them, maintaining social stability in their own countries is more important than expensive preparations for a military conflict between NATO and Russia.

And since countries like Germany, France, Italy and the United Kingdom cannot commit to a substantial increase in their defence budgets, gaps remain in terms of ammunition procurement, logistics, and digital capabilities, especially communications.

There is also a noticeable failure to address the issue of NATO forces' capacity to expand – that is, the ability to quickly mobilize additional soldiers during a potential conflict with Russia. During Russia's war of aggression against Ukraine there was an agreement that, firstly, more active-duty soldiers were needed in the alliance's forces, and secondly, that the capacity to expand in case of conflict had to be ensured. Now, both aspects are being overlooked.

Even the formal announcement by the US administration that it will be reducing US troop numbers in Europe in the near future to focus on the Indo-Pacific region cannot persuade most NATO heads of state and government to substantially change their defence policy.

Therefore, it remains unclear whether the operational plans developed in 2023, detailing the defence of NATO territory against Russian aggression, could be adequately implemented. When NATO's Supreme Allied Commander Europe asks countries to designate specific units to cover various geographical zones, too many are extremely slow to respond. As an excuse, they mention the European units stationed in Ukraine as part of the UN monitoring mission, arguing that they are already providing deterrence to Russia on the ground. Deterrence on the eastern flank of the alliance, – that is, in the Baltics – is no longer so important.

Those at NATO headquarters in Brussels are highly concerned by this apathy in the European capitals. Many military planners fear that if conventional US military support is significantly reduced or even completely withdrawn due to a parallel conflict in the Indo-Pacific region, there won't be enough soldiers in Europe to survive a protracted conflict with Russia. Of course, some European politicians try to gloss over these military deficits and talk up capabilities. However, such talk is unlikely to convince Russia.

The German chancellor, in particular, never tires of emphasizing that Olaf Scholz's assurance in 2022 that Germany was ready to defend every square metre of NATO territory also applies to the current government. But when the frustrated staff officers at the German Defence Ministry are asked about this, they just shrug and ask, 'With what?'

Meanwhile, Russia's arms production is running at full speed. Every year, Russia manages to recruit and equip 150,000 soldiers to replenish its armed forces. The Russian defence industry can even drive forward high-technology developments, thanks to investment from China and India. This primarily concerns the construction of new frigates and fighter jets. Asked about this enormous armament programme, the Russian president Obmanshchikov replies that his country, which clearly has no aggressive intentions towards any other country, should of course be allowed to rebuild its army for the purposes of self-defence.

Military planners across Europe fear that, in the event of a large-scale conflict with Russia, European defence forces would have so many capability gaps that NATO territory could only be defended with considerable losses. At the same time, they highlight the extreme danger in NATO's visible weaknesses, pointing out that, from a Russian perspective, such vulnerabilities boost the chances of success for a limited military operation against a NATO member state.

However, these critical voices, mostly from the military, are dismissed, sometimes sharply, by political leaders. The general line is that work on the deterrent capabilities of NATO and its member states is continuing apace, and that Russia's armed forces need at least four to six years to reorganize themselves, if not longer. There are also voices from within governments urging policymakers to wait and see if the new Russian president turns out to be a moderate – someone who will turn the clocks back to how things used to be.

The decreasing willingness to implement the ambitious pronouncements from 2022 and 2023 is reinforced by a stagnating economy in most NATO countries. Nowhere can the population be persuaded to spend even more on defence and thus implement cuts in public services, pensions or welfare. The Central and Eastern European countries, as well as the Baltic states, are the only ones where the threat perception remains high. People there aren't falling for the new Russian president's charm offensive. They see what is happening in the Ukrainian territories annexed by Russia, and warn against repeating mistakes of the past. They warn that we are sleepwalking into the same trap as we were before 2022. But their warnings, just like Cassandra's prophecies, go largely unheeded.

Moscow

Strategy

The international community is watching Russia's new president with excitement and, in some cases, fascination. Obmanshchikov's various proposals for easing tensions between East and West are actively discussed in expert circles and among the broader public. Yet while his various speeches, interviews and state visits give the impression of a new era, a select group of men hold a covert meeting in Moscow at his bidding to discuss the country's future security strategy.

The group consists of the chief of staff of the Presidential Administration, who is a former general and Obmanshchikov's close confidant; the newly appointed Chief of the General Staff of the Russian Armed Forces, a Ukraine war veteran; the heads of the military intelligence service (GRU) and the internal security service (FSB); and Igor Palachov, a close associate of Vladimir Putin and the owner of a private security company that conducts covert operations worldwide on behalf of the Russian state. Their task, as the president puts it at their first meeting, is to look for ways and means of continuing Putin's political course. Russia, of course, cannot afford for its economy to be on a war footing for another three years or longer. Still, it is imperative that Russia expands its influence in its immediate surroundings, to reinforce its claim of being on a par with the US and China.

What most surprises the men listening to the president is his remark about being on an equal footing with China. Because in fact, since the war against Ukraine, Russia has been demoted to the junior partner in relations with the emerging Asian superpower. Of course, official communiqués still talk of the unbreakable friendship between the two countries, but the reality is different. Sanctions have severely damaged Russia's economy, leaving it highly dependent on imports from China, and Chinese companies are filling the gaps left by the withdrawal of Western ones. Years of negotiations over the Power of Siberia 2 pipeline, intended to transport Russian gas to China, have ended in a deal. But the Chinese managed to push through advantageous prices for themselves, with Russia forced to reluctantly deliver its gas to China at relatively low prices. Talk of Russia as China's cheap petrol station is doing the rounds.

The challenge facing the elite group is to develop a strategy that does not lead directly to an open confrontation with NATO. 'Because,' as the chief of the general staff shares at a later meeting, without the president, 'although we have made good progress on rebuilding our army, we are still inferior to NATO in many conventional capabilities. We cannot risk a situation where NATO is able to react quickly and decisively.'

'In my view,' says the head of the GRU, 'the West has multiple weaknesses. Firstly, its efforts to build up and equip its army have stalled. Secondly, it doesn't look like either the political elites or the general public would be prepared to pay a high price once again, after years of supporting Ukraine, even to defend small territories within NATO's area of responsibility. And finally, the fear of nuclear escalation is still very high, particularly in Germany. Admittedly, these points do not apply to Central and Eastern European countries to the same extent as they do to "old Europe" and the US. But these countries alone, in our assessment, would not be able to defend the territory of a small European NATO member over a long period of time.'

'Politically, it would be enough to show the West its own inability to act,' counters Palachov. 'That will in itself cause considerable damage to the alliance. If that is the outcome of our operation, my dear friends, then we could call it a success.'

They all agree on one thing: they have been entrusted with a highly risky mission. They cannot afford to make the same mistake again as in the run-up to the February 2022 'special military operation'. Back then, Putin was presented with spurious reports to fulfil his desire to launch an operation and to persuade him it would all be over relatively quickly, because large parts of Ukraine's population would see Russia's invasion as a liberation, and the West was supposedly too weak and divided to summon any kind of firm response.

Those at the meeting agree that they can't now take a similar approach to the way they amassed troops on the border throughout 2021. The chief of the general staff summarizes the situation: 'We can't order a major military exercise, then keep troops in the region bordering the Baltic states, while making political demands of Washington. Any major troop movement on our part would immediately be perceived by NATO and the US as a repeat of 2021, and would be met with political, military and economic retaliation.'

He continues, 'Nor would we have secure grounds to hope that renewed military action from our side against another state would automatically be supported by our key allies, such as China and India, especially if such a conflict drags on.'

Even during the 'operation' in Ukraine, India was only partially on Russia's side, and only because it benefitted from the oil embargo. And the government in Beijing was getting exasperated that Russia could not manage to end the operation more quickly and decisively in its favour.

'Another aspect we need to keep in mind,' adds the head of the FSB, 'is the mood of our population. Not that I fear serious opposition to a new military campaign – our control of the opposition is too tight for that – but this time, it is important to prepare the population psychologically for the necessity of such an operation for the good of the Motherland.'

'So, the question is,' Palachov says, nudging the discussion on, 'how can we develop a campaign under such conditions that would not result in a massive Russian defeat or even a third world war?'

There is a moment of hesitation, interrupted by the president's chief of staff. Recalling his military training, he surprises the group with the following suggestion: 'Why don't we take the remilitarization of the Rhineland as a blueprint?'

'The remilitarization of the Rhineland?' Palachov asks in astonishment. 'What do you mean by that?'

The former general looks around the room, clearly pleased to have the chance to give the others a little history lesson. 'The German region of the Rhineland was demilitarized according to the Treaty of Versailles in 1919,' he begins. 'The French in particular feared that the presence of German troops in the Rhineland would jeopardize their security. Nevertheless, on 7 March 1936, 30,000 Wehrmacht soldiers marched over bridges across the Rhine to remilitarize the Rhineland area. As justification, Hitler cited the Franco-Soviet mutual assistance treaty ratified in February of that year. The Nazis' plan was to withdraw immediately if there was any resistance to the remilitarization – but if there was none, to remain. At the same time, the advance of German troops was accompanied by peaceful rhetoric from the Nazis, an insistence that Nazi Germany had no aggressive intentions towards its neighbours. Surprisingly, the UK believed this and did not react to this incursion; neither did France. And so the Wehrmacht remained in the Rhineland.

'So, the aim of a Russian campaign,' he continues, 'should be to test the readiness of NATO states to respond to a Russian advance. Such a campaign needs to be accompanied by rhetoric that makes it clear from the outset that the advance of Russian troops is focused only on a limited area and that we have no ambitions beyond that. If, contrary to our expectations, there is a quick response from NATO, we can cancel the operation and swiftly withdraw from the captured territory to save face.

'We will need to use the element of surprise. On the one hand, we cannot wait for our armed forces to be fully replenished, because that would also give NATO states the time to close their capability gaps. In the event of an unlikely, but not inconceivable, united response from NATO to Russia's actions, we would immediately be at a disadvantage. To avoid this, we will need to create a situation where individual NATO states, especially the US, are temporarily distracted from actual events on the ground.'

This idea finds support among everyone at the meeting. They leave with an agreement to work out a concrete strategy along this framework and to meet again to discuss the details. It is also agreed that these discussions must remain restricted to a very close circle, and that the plan should only be presented to the president once it is unanimously agreed. The president's chief of staff promises to inform the president about the meeting but without going into specific details.

Kidal, Mali

2 February 2028: The game is on

It is a chilly evening, not as hot and humid as usual, when Anaya sets off for home. She has been running some errands after work and is now on her way back to her husband, Abdoulaye, and their three children. Their house is in a suburb of Kidal in northern Mali, a city that has been through a lot in recent years. First, it was a jihadi stronghold; then it was recaptured by government troops around 2024 and brought under their control. Of the 25,000-strong population, more than a third have fled. Some went to the south of the country, aiming for Bamako, the capital. Others went straight to neighbouring Algeria, where security forces put them in refugee camps. Anaya and her family stayed; they hope to hold out until the horror of the war ends at some point.

Things have been quieter since the Malian army regained control of the city. Although there are still isolated battles between government forces and jihadists in the surrounding area, the massacres that groups with links to Al-Qaeda and Islamic State used to carry out against the civilian population seem to be a thing of the past. All this has helped Anaya, an employee at the city administration, feel more confident in her decision to stay in Kidal with her family, and not to flee the city like so many of her acquaintances and relatives have. She and Abdoulaye, like many other residents, were taken aback when Russian-speaking men in uniforms began to patrol the city streets alongside Malian government troops. But so far they haven't been too worried, assuming that it will improve their chances of living in safety.

That is, until this chilly evening when so much will change – and not just in Anaya's life.

At first, it is only the sounds of passing vehicles that confuse her. Usually there isn't this much traffic in the evening in their neighbourhood. But once she's home she doesn't give it much thought, because she is busy with the usual chores of family life. It is only when she hears loud screams that she asks her husband to go to the window to have a look.

What Abdoulaye sees down on the street is very worrying: large, open-backed trucks carrying numerous armed Malian soldiers and a few Russian mercenaries, recognizable by their uniforms. They stop, the soldiers jump out and force their way into houses. They're shouting as they drive Anaya's neighbours

– men, women, children; old and young – out onto the street. They then force them at gunpoint onto the backs of the trucks, which are khaki green and clearly military vehicles. They call at every house on the street. Abdoulaye glances to the right and sees the same is happening on a side street.

'I don't know what's happening,' he says to Anaya, 'but we need to get out of here, now.'

She looks at him in disbelief.

'They're rounding everyone up from their homes. We have to leave – now!'

Anaya is frozen to the spot. Peace has only just returned to her town, and the fighting had stopped. This can't be happening.

'What is this?' she thinks frantically.

But as thoughts race through her mind, she feels Abdoulaye's hand grab her firmly by the forearm as he pulls her and the children along behind him, down the stairs from the third floor. As they reach the front door and step outside, they are met by the glare of headlights. A truck is parked directly outside their door. In the blinding light, they can vaguely make out the shapes of guns pointed at them. They hear frantic shouting.

They have been travelling for hours in the back of the truck, with people crammed in like animals being transported to slaughter, when the vehicle comes to a halt. A jumble of voices can be heard outside. They can barely understand a word. Some words of Arabic, fragments of another foreign language, some snippets of something European-sounding. It is stuffy in the back of the truck. It stinks of sweat, urine and faeces. Anaya has lost all sense of time. Have they been travelling for eight or fifteen hours? She cannot say. In the mass of bodies, she's drifted in and out of sleep, terrified about what might happen to her and her children. Abdoulaye has been crouched next to them the whole time, but he isn't much comfort. His fear seems even more palpable than hers.

Anaya wonders why the truck has stopped. Will they be handed over to someone else, perhaps even Mauritanian slave traders? She's heard stories of people being abducted and taken to Mauritania to work as slaves. Or could this be linked to the Islamic State slave markets she's heard still exist, where women and men are sold to jihadist terrorists?

After what feels like an eternity, the tarpaulin covering the back of the truck is suddenly pulled back. Bright lights are shone into the vehicle, making it hard to see the people standing outside. She can only hear the shouts in English: 'Out, out, out!' and 'Go, go, go!' As she jumps down from the truck, her eyes slowly adjust to the darkness, and she realises that they have ended up somewhere in the middle of the desert. She sees hundreds of people streaming out of numerous trucks. Men – some in uniform, some not – are rounding them up at gunpoint. She guesses that there must be between 300 and 400 people gathered here. She still has no idea why. Now, besides the fear of slavery, there's also the terror of being shot.

A somewhat heavy-set man in military uniform, clearly not an African or an Arab, steps in front of the crowd. Next to him is a slightly gaunt man of African descent in civilian clothing, who serves as his interpreter.

'From here,' says the stout man, 'we will take you to the coast, where you will board boats to Europe. Anyone who resists will face immediate consequences.'

He then turns to the armed soldiers standing behind him and gives some kind of command. They step closer to the people they have rounded up and scream at them to start moving.

After walking for over a day, they can smell the salty air coming from the sea. However, they have been brought not to a harbour, but to a simple beach. There, they are forced to board narrow wooden boats that take them to several ships anchored off the coast. The crews are of Arab origin. Once on board one of these ships, Anaya is crammed into the lower deck with her family and most of the other captives. The few who cannot fit in the hull remain on the upper deck. And then the ships set sail.

Brussels

5 February 2028: Europe takes the bait

The latest wave of refugees heading towards Europe from the southern shore of the Mediterranean does not go unnoticed for long. Every day, up to 500 people arrive in Malta or one of the Canary Islands. This is an alternative route, as the island of Lampedusa is now well guarded by the Italian navy and police.

At the same time, various news agencies report that their sources in the Middle East and North Africa are once again observing Russian and Belarusian embassies issuing visas en masse to Syrians, Afghans, Iraqis and Sudanese nationals, who are then able to purchase tickets to Moscow and Minsk for relatively low prices. This brings back memories of 2021, when Belarus attempted to smuggle several thousand refugees into Poland.

There is a strong sense of urgency at the EU's Foreign Affairs Council. At its emergency meeting on 5 February 2028, the Council decides to deploy a rapid response force and to strengthen the role of Frontex, the European border police. Germany joins France, Italy and Spain in pledging two frigates to the MEDMARFOR (Mediterranean Maritime Force) rapid reaction force to tackle illegal migration in the Mediterranean.

Sceptics in the German Ministry of Defence point out that deploying the frigates will dangerously weaken the protection of the Baltic Sea. Without them, the German navy will be unable to fulfil its commitments within the framework of NATO's defence plans. But these warnings are ignored by politicians. Germany has recently seen a significant fall in the number of refugees, since the government started systematically sending them back: to Ukraine, but also to Syria, where a government formed after the fall of Assad that is Islamist but respects at least some basic human rights. No one wants to risk the numbers skyrocketing again, as this would only strengthen the far-right and left-wing fringes in Germany. German politicians therefore argue that there is no option but to participate in this mission, for reasons of both domestic and foreign policy.

South China Sea

28 February 2028: Help from an ally

Tensions between the Philippines and China have reached new heights by the end of February. The conflict centres on Second Thomas Shoal in the South China Sea, a reef disputed because of the substantial oil, gas and rare earth deposits the surrounding area is believed to contain. When the Philippines is forced to temporarily evacuate its small provisional garrison on the reef in the wake of a typhoon, China immediately dispatches armed forces there and stations autonomous underwater systems to monitor the area. Satellite images provided to the Philippines by the US government also show that China has brought a dozen soldiers and construction workers to the reef and is installing a radar system.

In response to China's actions, the Philippines dispatches its coast guard with a patrol boat to assert its claims and restore territorial control. However, China has already established a maritime exclusion zone around the reef.

China's takeover is backed by an aggressive social media campaign. Thousands of fake accounts are supporting the official Chinese propaganda channels in arguing that the reef historically belongs to China and that sending Chinese soldiers and establishing a maritime exclusion zone is purely a defensive measure against the Philippines' long-standing illegal influence in the region. This aggressive campaign, to which Philippine diplomacy has little to offer in response, is making itself felt across Southeast Asia. While the public mood is still very pro-Philippines in the first few days, it shifts towards a greater understanding of China's actions.

In their hour of need, the Philippines asks its most important ally, the United States, for military and diplomatic support. Although there is little appetite in the White House to risk direct military confrontation with China over a reef in the South China Sea, Washington does feel obliged to respond in some way; firstly, because of the bilateral defence agreement between the Philippines and the US, and secondly, because it sees the danger of the floodgates opening if the Chinese get away with this provocation. However, in discussions between the US president and his national security advisor, there is initial disagreement as to whether the response to China's occupation of the reef should be tough from the outset or more restrained. There is agreement, however, that the *George Washington* carrier strike group will be sent into international waters and a protest will be lodged with the Chinese government via the US ambassador in Beijing.

They also discuss other measures, such as offensive cyber operations to disrupt China's logistics and communications, and the deployment of underwater drones equipped with sensors to monitor China's underwater activity. But the fear that China might then be tempted to escalate further and threaten Taiwan speaks against a more aggressive approach. Naysayers within the National Security Council worry that such a move could cause the situation to spiral out of control. Given that China is the world's third-largest nuclear power, such a course of action would not be advisable.

While the White House is still searching for an appropriate strategy, the situation at Second Thomas Shoal escalates. During an attempt by the Philippine Navy to enforce the island nation's territorial claims, a Chinese ship fires a water cannon at a Philippine coast guard boat, rendering it unmanoeuvrable; another boat that enters China's newly declared maritime exclusion zone is rammed so hard by a Chinese coast guard vessel that it sinks. However, all Filipino sailors and soldiers on board are rescued.

Meanwhile, a communications battle is raging on social media, stirring up nationalist sentiment in both countries. In particular, a deepfake video of the Philippine defence minister threatening the Chinese with massive retaliation for sinking the patrol boat is fuelling tensions on both sides.

The regional organization ASEAN, which was asked by the Philippines to mediate in the conflict during an emergency meeting, has been unable to issue a clear statement. China's influence over countries such as Cambodia and Laos is too great for them to oppose China, and other Southeast Asian countries, such as Malaysia and Myanmar, prefer not to take any position in this conflict.

All appeals by the Philippines to the Chinese side to resolve the conflict through diplomacy have been fruitless. On the contrary, China is ratcheting up the pressure. In its efforts to keep the US out of the conflict, it is forging ahead with the fortification of Second Thomas Shoal and sending two nuclear submarines to the Taiwan Strait under the pretext of military exercises.

The US responds to this escalation with a two-pronged approach. First, it establishes a secret channel of communication with the Chinese government and party leadership, through its UN ambassador. The US does not inform the Philippine government about this channel, let alone involve them. At the same time, the US dispatches another carrier strike group to international waters. Although the White House's official line is that no options are being ruled out, in view of China's escalating aggression, Beijing interprets the willingness to resolve the conflict through secret talks and without the involvement of the Philippines as a sign of weakness. The Chinese state and party leadership understands from this that the US is not prepared to go to war over a reef.

In Russia, the crisis in the South China Sea is met with jubilation. Of course, Russia asked its Chinese allies to create a diversion to distract attention from NATO's eastern flank. But that China would go so far as to make its own interests in the Taiwan Strait the subject of this diversion, as it has done by deploying nuclear submarines, is more than anyone could have dreamed of.

Seattle

27 March 2028, 01:00 UTC

It is around 6 p.m. local time on 26 March 2028 when the US president, attending the annual conference of American electricity providers at a hotel in Seattle, is handed his secure cryptophone by his personal assistant. 'Mr President, the director of the CIA for you.' The president immediately retreats to a private corner, surrounded by his advisors, to take the call.

'What's so urgent?' he snaps. 'Why are you calling me on this line?'

'Mr President, we have satellite images and have confirmed reports on the ground that Russian units are on their way to Narva, Estonia, and that several speedboats are crossing the river. We have also intercepted radio communications from Russia's Baltic Fleet indicating that a medium-scale operation is about to begin. However, our analysts are unsure of the objective and the direction from which they are approaching.'

'Have the defence secretary and the secretary of state been informed?'

'No, sir,' replies the CIA director.

'Then go and tell them,' comes the president's terse command.

After handing back the mobile phone, he turns to one of his staff. 'I need to call the German chancellor, the British prime minister, the French president and the NATO secretary general. Set me up with a secure line. But first, I need a video call with the secretary of state, the defence secretary, the chairman of the Joint Chiefs of Staff, the national security advisor and the director of the CIA.'

It takes a while before the president can begin his meeting with his closest national security team. First, all parties need to be taken to secure rooms, which proves somewhat difficult in the case of the secretary of state, who is on an official visit to Chile. The only secure room trusted by the CIA is at the US embassy in Santiago.

The president begins the meeting by sharing the intel from the CIA, which everyone else has also received by now. He then asks those present for their assessment of the situation.

First, he invites his national security advisor to speak. He clears his throat and begins: 'We are most likely dealing with a limited attack by Russia on a NATO member state. At the moment, there are no indications of any major troop movements that would suggest a large-scale invasion. However,' he adds, 'we don't know what surprises Russia has in store. In this respect, the next few hours will be critical.'

'What are our options?' the president asks the defence secretary.

'We have approximately 700 troops stationed in Estonia who we could deploy to recapture the territory. Together with the 1,700 NATO troops, we should be able to overcome any threat, provided the Russians don't send in massive reinforcements. And provided they don't deploy their air force and missiles against us.'

The chair of the Joint Chiefs of Staff interrupts unprompted. 'If we did this, Mr President, it would be a direct military confrontation between NATO and Russia. We would then have to destroy targets in Russia with our cruise missiles to prevent a build-up of additional Russian troops. Or Russia might fire ballistic missiles at targets in Europe.'

'We would be at war with Russia?' the president checks. 'We're talking World War III?'

'Yes, sir,' replies the top US military officer, and everyone else on the screen nods.

'But if we do nothing, Mr President,' the secretary of state interjects, 'we'll have lost. America's credibility would suffer in the eyes of our allies – not just in Europe, but also in Asia. It would strengthen the Axis of Revisionists.'

The secretary of state has taken to using the term 'Axis of Revisionists' in his speeches lately when referring to the connection between countries such as Russia, China, North Korea and Iran. He accuses them of wanting to undermine the US-dominated international order.

'What options do we have short of a direct military response?' the president asks the virtual gathering.

'Not many,' replies the national security advisor.

'But what?' comes the visibly annoyed response. 'Tell me!'

'Well...' The advisor takes a deep breath. 'We could move the Second Fleet to the Baltic Sea region and put the armed forces on high alert to signal to the Russians that we are ready for anything.'

The CIA director immediately adds, 'But to avoid Russia seeing all this as preparation for a full-scale attack, we need to communicate with the Russians. Nothing is more dangerous in such a situation than a misunderstanding.'

'I'm supposed to call Obmanshchikov?' asks the president, looking puzzled. 'I've never even met the guy.'

'No, sir, you don't have to do it yourself. At least, not yet,' replies the national security advisor. 'We will try to pursue other channels first. But if that doesn't work, then I think, yes, sir, you will have to pick up the phone.'

The president ends the video conference with a command to the military to work through the options they discussed and then, before they are implemented, to 'cushion' them through direct communication channels with Moscow.

His next conference call is in just two hours. It is with the heads of state and government of America's most important allies within NATO, as well as the NATO secretary general. The president is clear on the most important message he wants to convey to them. He is not about to risk a Third World War over a small Estonian town, but he is prepared to exert military pressure on Russia to withdraw its troops.

Berlin

27 March 2028, 02:20 UTC

News of the Russian attack has spread like wildfire. It is the top news bulletin on all the German TV channels, most of which begin broadcasting special reports in the early hours of the morning.

The German chancellor is spending the night in a hotel in Frankfurt, where he gave the opening address at a major Deutsche Bank conference the evening before. He is woken up at 4.20 a.m. local time by a phone call from his chief of staff, who informs him of the Russian attack. Shortly afterwards, he is already on his way to the Frankfurt police headquarters, where a military helicopter is waiting to take him to Berlin. During the roughly two-hour flight to the capital, the chancellor tries to get an overview of the situation – as much as is possible while sitting in a helicopter. The dossiers hastily put together for him don't contain much new information. And since his engagement the previous evening was at a finance industry event, he is accompanied only by his office manager, the government press secretary and the head of financial policy at the Federal Chancellery. This means the chancellor will have to wait until he arrives in Berlin before he has access to all-source intelligence.

When the helicopter lands at the helipad of the Federal Chancellery at 7.19 a.m., the chancellor is greeted by his chief of staff, the national security advisor and the inspector general of the German armed forces. On the short walk to the Federal Chancellery and then up to the seventh floor, where the chancellor's office is located, the three men try to fill him in on the latest developments. The most important update is that a video conference with the presidents of the United States and France, the British prime minister and the NATO secretary general is scheduled to take place in about an hour.

While the German chancellor is in his office discussing the situation with his key advisors, the CEO of Germany's largest arms manufacturer gets into his armoured limousine approximately 600 kilometres west of Berlin, to drive to the airport, where he will board a business jet to Berlin. In the middle of the night, the head of the Directorate General for Armament within the Federal Ministry of Defence asked the top CEOs in the German arms industry to drop everything and come to Berlin for an urgent meeting. The vice admiral who heads the department knows full well that this may be about putting the German economy on a long-term war footing. For security reasons, he insists on a face-to-face meeting and does not want to hold a video or telephone conference, fearing that these could be intercepted by foreign intelligence services.

So the CEO of Ruhreisen, Europe's leading manufacturer of armoured vehicles and tanks, immediately sets off for the airport. Once there, he boards the Gulfstream G650 executive jet that is already waiting for him. He takes off his jacket, asks the steward to bring him a coffee, and takes a stack of papers out of his leather briefcase, which he intends to at least skim through during the short flight to Berlin.

He is so focused on the papers in front of him that he doesn't even notice when the pilot starts the engines and, after a brief pause, the aircraft begins to taxi towards the runway. The Gulfstream then accelerates down the runway until the pilot adjusts the elevator to lift the nose of the aircraft.

As the CEO reaches for his coffee, he takes a moment to glance out of the oval window up at the sky. The sun is shining in his face, causing him to squint for a moment, so he doesn't see an elongated object approaching the aircraft at breakneck speed.

The object, a Stinger missile, hits one of the engines, and within seconds the Gulfstream is out of control.

As if by an invisible hand, its ascent is halted, and after a moment when it would seem to an onlooker as if it were suspended in mid-air, the aircraft falls like a stone to the ground, breaks apart and bursts into flames.

The news of the plane crash reaches the chancellor during his meeting with the heads of the intelligence services. And although there is no knowing who is behind the attack, everyone in the room is convinced there can only be one culprit: the Kremlin.

The chancellor was close to the CEO of the arms company. They had known each for over twenty years. But there's no time to mourn or give free rein to his feelings for his 'friend', if such a thing even exists in politics. The phone call to his bereaved family will have to wait until the evening, if it happens at all. Because now it is time to discuss how to respond to the Russian attack.

Berlin

27 March 2028, 06:30 UTC

The German chancellor enters the virtual meeting a little late, and the presidents of the United States and France and the NATO secretary general are already waiting. For some reason, the British prime minister has not joined yet.

The US president starts the meeting all the same. There is no time to waste.

'Gentlemen, as you all know, Russian troops took control of the Estonian city of Narva and the island of Hiiumaa off the coast of Estonia this morning. Our intelligence services are reporting troop movements in Russia towards the Baltic states. We are also seeing increased activity by the Russian navy in St Petersburg and in Kaliningrad. I requested this meeting because I want to discuss how we respond to these developments.'

After a few seconds of silence, the French president speaks up. 'The situation is very unclear. Do we know what Russia's goal is?'

'No, our intelligence services have no information about that,' replies the American president, 'but at first glance, it doesn't look like the Russian troop movements suggest a further wave of attacks. However, we can't rule out the possibility that Russia might set up a naval blockade off the coast of the Baltic states. Perhaps the secretary general can tell us what consequences that would have?'

'Sure,' he says, joining the discussion. He is sitting in his spacious Brussels office, with the chairman of the NATO Military Committee at his side. 'If Russia imposes a naval blockade on the Baltic states in the next twenty-four hours, it will take our Tier 1 troops at least ten days to reach the Baltic region.'

'Tier 1 troops are the 100,000 men and women whom NATO can deploy to the Baltics within ten days to form the first line of defence,' whispers the US national security advisor to the president.

'Do you think I don't know that?' he snaps back.

'These troops could no longer be transported via the Baltic Sea,' the NATO secretary general continues, 'but would have to pass through the Suwałki Gap instead, where they would be exposed to the constant threat of Russian attacks from Kaliningrad and also from Belarus.'

'The Suwałki Gap is a narrow land corridor between Kaliningrad and Belarus, and the only route for our troops to get directly from Poland to Lithuania…' The national security advisor falls silent when the US president glares at him.

'For us, this would mean ...' the secretary general begins, when suddenly the British prime minister appears on the screen.

'Gentlemen, sincere apologies for my delay,' he says, slightly out of breath. 'There's been a series of explosions at our naval base at Faslane, HMNB Clyde. No one has been killed, but parts of the infrastructure there have been severely damaged. As you all know, this is where our nuclear submarines are based. I therefore considered it my national duty to respond to those events first.'

'Any information about the perpetrators that you can share with us?' asks the German chancellor.

'No, none,' replies the prime minister. 'But our intelligence services suspect sabotage.'

'We are dealing with a hybrid war,' the chancellor concludes. 'It has been waged against our countries and societies for some time but is now becoming increasingly intense. In Germany, a leading CEO in the defence industry has just been killed in an attack. We also don't know anything yet about the perpetrators, but without pre-empting the investigation, I think it is reasonable to assume that Russia or a state friendly to Russia is behind it.'

'Perhaps we could now give the floor back to the secretary general,' urges the US president.

'Gladly,' the secretary general starts again. 'So, if Russia were to impose a naval blockade, we would be forced to transfer our troops through the Suwałki Gap, which would expose them to considerable risk, or we would have to break the naval blockade, which would mean that we would then be directly at war with Russia.'

'What could Russia's goal be?' the French president asks the meeting. 'Surely they can't mean to start a war with NATO? Maybe they want to protect the Russians in Estonia? It must be noted that Estonia has not fully respected their rights for years…'

'It doesn't matter what Russia's goals are, it has attacked NATO territory,' the German chancellor replies. 'We cannot allow such an act of provocation to go unanswered. I think–'

'I have asked the army to work out different options for a response,' interrupts the US president, 'which after consulting with you, we will, of course' – here the French president sneers at the German chancellor – 'clearly communicate to the Russians.

'The Estonians are going to demand a consultation on the basis of Article 5 of the NATO Treaty,' he continues. 'Sure. We can't say no to that, but we should go into talks with a unified position, where possible. But let me be clear: I'm not going to risk World War III over some small town in Estonia. Unless we have concrete evidence that Obmanshchikov wants to seize more territory, I will not, and the United States will not, agree to invoke Article 5.

'I suggest,' the American president adds, 'that our foreign and defence ministers and national security advisors stay in touch to coordinate further. But we need to move fast.'

And that concludes the meeting. Once all participants have left the virtual room, the German chancellor turns to his security advisor and says, 'If NATO doesn't respond, Russia has won. I hope everyone realizes that.'

Moscow

27 March 2028, 07:00 UTC

The mood is serious but not tense as President Obmanshchikov has a morning meeting with his closest advisors in the Kremlin. Everyone present knows that they have succeeded in pulling off a surprise, but that it is impossible to predict what consequences this coup will have in the coming days.

Obmanshchikov opens the meeting and starts by praising those present. 'Gentlemen, I must take this opportunity to pay you a great compliment. Your plan...' He turns his head towards his chief of staff. 'Well, I was a little sceptical at first, but now I have to say: it has worked.'

Applause breaks out.

'We have not only taken them by surprise, we've also caused a great deal of confusion. Everyone is shocked but no one knows what we are up to. And that makes it difficult for the imperialist forces to respond. We will now need to think through our next steps carefully.

We're faced with a delicate balance between our goal of reshaping the European security architecture and avoiding a full-scale confrontation with the United States and its NATO vassals.'

Everybody nods in agreement.

'For this reason,' the president continues, 'I spoke with President Xi yesterday, thanking him for the valuable assistance in tying up part of the US armed forces in Asia. I assured him that we won't be needing to call on his help any more. He agreed with me that Russian-Chinese friendship is unbreakable and that we are moving ever closer to our common goal of a peaceful system that is fair to all nations.'

Obmanshchikov pauses, looks around the room, and after a few seconds asks in a quiet but very determined voice: 'How do we proceed? What options do we have?'

The head of the GRU is the first to break the silence. 'Control and escalation should be the principles guiding our further actions.' And since he notices that some people don't fully understand what he means, he adds, 'We all agree that we can't afford a major conflict with NATO at the moment. Our armed forces are not yet ready after our glorious special military operation in Ukraine. But this is, of course, not information we should give to the enemy. The enemy should believe the opposite. So what I am saying is this: in order to avoid a major conflict, we should let the enemy know that our goals are limited. That we have no intention of challenging NATO as such. However, to prevent the enemy side from recognizing our weakness and therefore standing their ground, we also need a strategy that puts them under pressure, that makes them believe that if they want this confrontation, we will not shy away from it. That is what I mean by control and escalation – or, more precisely, escalation for the sake of control.'

'That is all very well, but if you continue to escalate, you could quickly lose control,' argues the head of the FSB, visibly peeved that he didn't get to make the first proposal. 'The two ideas are essentially contradictory.'

'Not really,' comes the bemused reply from the GRU chief. 'This is about psychology. If we simply communicate that our goals are limited, the West will sense weakness. What if they decide to strike back? NATO has troops in Estonia. What if they drive our soldiers out? The West will want to back down if they sense that a counterattack would risk starting World War III, and seeing that our goals are limited gives them a route out of a retaliation without losing face. The current stakes are too low to risk a world war.

'To leave no doubt about our resolve and to show that we are ready and not afraid of confrontation, we need to cause even more confusion. China is currently distracting the US in Asia, and our guys in Africa have managed to keep the European naval forces busy in the Mediterranean. Where is NATO's next weak point? Where would they least expect a limited action – where we don't need to fire at NATO forces, but can still show the world we mean business?'

'Your plan depends entirely on the West thinking we're schizophrenic,' the FSB chief persists. 'That they believe us when we say we don't really want a major confrontation, even though our actions are provoking one. It's a dangerous balancing act. If it goes wrong, either we will have to back down, like that wimp Khrushchev in 1962 during the Cuban Missile Crisis, or we will have to fight a battle we cannot win. So what is your communication strategy? The same as Hitler's? A combination of aggression and public rhetoric about peace? Isn't that a bit simplistic?'

'Not at all,' says the head of the GRU. 'We need to remember: the West thinks that they are rational, and that we are irrational and emotionally backward. Imperial fossils who are capable of anything. That's to our advantage. They will take our schizophrenia at face value, because it fits their image of us. But you're right, relying on public communication would be risky. We should first use our unofficial, confidential channels, to convey to Western government leaders that while we don't want conflict, we're not afraid of it either. You'll see: there will be a whole host of high-ranking Western politicians who will do our work for us and influence public opinion in our favour. This worked well during our special military operation, after all. And if we don't make everything public, it also has the advantage that we don't expose the US president. Instead, we give him the chance to sell a possible reaction in our favour as his own idea.'

'As we know,' the president's chief of staff interrupts, 'he doesn't want to look like he's lost, even though it's obvious.'

For the first time, something resembling cheerfulness fills the room. Everyone has a good chuckle.

When the room has quietened down again, President Obmanshchikov turns to the chief of the general staff. 'Then tell me: where does NATO have another "soft underbelly", as Churchill put it? Where could we strike without major effort and without either side suffering casualties?'

The chief of the general staff needs a moment to think. Of course, he and his team have already thought through this precise question. After all, strategy is at the heart of what the military does. Several options have been considered. The idea of a limited incursion into northern Finland using the forces of the Leningrad Military District, reconstituted in 2024, was rejected fairly quickly. Although this would be relatively easy to achieve, occupying the heartland of a second NATO member state would be politically very risky.

But uninhabited or sparsely populated islands are a different story. And there are quite a few of those.

Spitsbergen, for example, in Norway, where there were two Russian colonies until 2000. Or Hans Island, which Denmark and Canada fought over for decades before it was finally split between the two countries. It is only about 1.3 square kilometres in size, uninhabited, with no known natural resources. Nevertheless, 'capturing' this barren rock in the Nares Strait between Canada's Ellesmere Island and Greenland would be an impressive demonstration of the power projection capability of the Russian navy. Moreover, NATO would certainly not expect an 'attack' on an island between Canada and Greenland.

'We could,' the chief of the general staff finally begins, 'take a submarine to an uninhabited island, and drop off a few Spetsnaz guys who can raise the Russian flag and then disappear again. Hans Island is a possibility. This could be the most effective measure to show our resolve without directly provoking the enemy into a response.'

The meeting participants nod in agreement.

'What about our anti-satellite weapon in space?' asks the president's chief of staff. 'Could we use that?'

'We could,' replies the chief of the general staff, 'but then we would shut down all communications in every country that has satellites in space, including our own. We might as well attack the US directly with nuclear weapons,' he adds ironically. 'That's more something we can save as a threat, to show we mean business.'

'I would like to pick up on that point,' says Putin's confidant Palachov, who has contributed little to the talks so far, although his standing has risen sharply thanks to the successful operation by his mercenaries in Mali. 'The West, its elites and its population are afraid of nuclear weapons – irrationally afraid. We saw that during the special military operation against the Ukrainian fascists. Whenever President Putin or one of his close advisors threatened to use nuclear weapons, Western Europe was horrified, and our friends in various countries who warned against escalation gained prominence in the public discourse. That's why politicians like Scholz and Biden were hamstrung in their policy of supporting our enemy. It was precisely because they took our willingness to use nuclear weapons seriously that our threats were so effective.'

President Obmanshchikov, who has listened quietly to his advisors' discussion and taken notes throughout, attempts to bring things to a close. 'I agree with you, gentlemen. We must show that we mean business without going too far. The idea of occupying an uninhabited island has its charm. At the same time, I will ask our ambassador to the United Nations to contact the US president's security advisor to convey our determination, but also our limited objectives. Then we'll take it from there.'

NATO Headquarters, Brussels

27 March 2028, 12:00 UTC

At NATO headquarters – a light-filled glass building with a design reminiscent of interlocking fingers forming a unified whole – the thirty-two permanent representatives of the NATO member states convene for an emergency meeting called by the secretary general. The meeting is held in Room 1, directly to the left of the airy main entrance. The members of the NATO Military Committee and the two strategic commanders of NATO, the Supreme Allied Commander Europe and the Supreme Allied Commander Transformation, based in Norfolk, in the US, have also been invited to attend the meeting. The only item on the agenda is the Russian aggression against Estonia.

The secretary general begins the meeting by presenting the facts, and concludes with the Estonian prime minister's request, already known to those present, to convene a formal North Atlantic Council meeting at the level of heads of state and government, with the intention of invoking Article 5 of the North Atlantic Treaty.

'I have asked you to come here today,' the secretary general explains, 'to get an overview of your governments' stances. I am well aware that not all, or perhaps none, of the member states of our alliance will have a definitive opinion on Estonia's request. All the same, we shouldn't squander this opportunity to exchange perspectives. I have also invited to this meeting the representatives of the Military Committee, including the commanders of the two strategic NATO commands, to provide military advice where needed.'

The secretary general looks around expectantly at the ambassadors.

The Polish representative is the first to speak. 'Ladies and gentlemen, on behalf of my government, I can tell you that Poland is of the view that this Russian aggression against a NATO member state must be met with a decisive response. We cannot and must not accept a violation of the territorial integrity of the alliance, even if it is only a small piece of land. We are familiar with Russian imperialism and know its goals. It will not stop at this provocation. If we do not now resolutely defend every square metre of our allied territory, to quote the former German chancellor Olaf Scholz' – her lips turn up in a slightly ironic smile – 'it will be the end of the NATO alliance. If we cannot rely on Article 5 in an emergency, what is the point of the treaty?'

The Italian ambassador is next to address the group. 'Don't shoot the messenger,' he begins, 'but we do not yet have enough information to make a final assessment of the situation. Yes, we have the attacks in Germany and the United Kingdom, and we have the limited aggression against Estonia. But what is also true' – here he looks directly at the Estonian ambassador – 'is that the Estonian government has not been particularly prudent in the past with regard to protecting the minority rights of Russians living within its territory.'

'Mr Chairman,' the Estonian representative interjects. 'I would like to make a firm rebuttal of this assertion. The Russian-speaking minority in our country has the same rights, but also the same duties, as every Estonian citizen. What we are currently experiencing is an act of aggression against our country and a violation of our territorial integrity, to which there can be only one response.'

However, the Italian representative is not alone in his call for caution. The Southern European members of the alliance express their solidarity with Estonia, but at the same time urge restraint in any response. The thrust of their contributions is that more information is needed about Russian intentions and military movements before they can make any real assessment of the situation.

The attitude of the Central and Eastern Europeans, the United Kingdom and the two other Baltic states is quite different. Their representatives emphasize two aspects already mentioned by the Polish ambassador. They argue that NATO cannot leave this test unanswered, as to do so would mean the alliance losing its core function. This is in all likelihood only the first step, and further military aggression by Russia is to be anticipated.

After almost everyone has spoken, Hungary's representative takes the floor. She also stresses that her government has not yet reached a final assessment, but as far as they are concerned 'a military conflict between NATO and Russia should be avoided at all costs'. She continues: 'We are talking here about a potential World War III that neither side can win. It would be crazy' – her precise words – 'if we were to trigger this by acting imprudently. In the view of my government, it would be better if the presidents of Russia and the United States were to finally sit down and discuss things on a larger scale. I am confident,' she says, concluding her brief statement, 'that such an approach would contribute more to the security of Estonia and Europe than an unnecessary military provocation on our part, which could end in the obliteration of humanity.'

During her remarks, the Slovak and French representatives to the Council can be seen nodding in agreement from time to time.

The German representative, who has only been in her position for six months, is the last to speak. When the secretary general gives her the floor, she says: 'For my government, one of the key questions, besides the assessment of Russia's intentions, is what our military options are. How quickly can we reach Estonian territory, and are there military options we can deploy without immediately triggering a major conflict with Russia? Perhaps the two strategic commanders could answer this question for us.'

The secretary general nods in agreement and turns to the two generals present. 'Gentlemen, please.'

'Gladly,' says the Supreme Allied Commander Europe, who is also commander of the United States Forces Command. 'Regardless of any political analysis of Russia's intentions, the situation is as follows. By capturing Hiiumaa, Russia could very swiftly establish a naval blockade around the Baltic states. This would isolate the forces we have on the ground. To break this blockade, we would have to deploy our maritime units, some of which have been stationed in the Mediterranean for some time as part of the EU-led mission to prevent irregular migration. But even then, we would have to be prepared to risk military conflict with Russia. Russia would likely support its naval forces from the air and attempt to escalate the situation elsewhere. Right now, I can only speculate as to what such an escalation might look like. But in all likelihood, it would involve firing ballistic missiles at European territory. We cannot say whether these would be nuclear or conventional warheads. The fact is, however, that we still do not have sufficient air capabilities for a far-reaching defence of allied territory against such an attack. It would be reasonable to assume that, were Russia to react in this way, the damage would be vast.

'We could of course pre-empt such a development by deploying weapons from the outset that can strike deep into Russian territory, destroying missile launchers, airfields and command centres. For this, we would use electronic warfare to disable Russian air defence systems and early warning radar systems. The result would be that Russia would see incoming missiles, but in the case of long-range hypersonic weapons such as Dark Eagle, they would be unable to determine whether they were equipped with conventional or nuclear warheads until they hit their target. This could prompt a nuclear response, even if we informed our counterparts in Moscow in advance through our channels that these missiles were only equipped with conventional warheads.'

These remarks are met with silence across the conference chamber. You could hear a pin drop. It was clear to all present at the start of the meeting what a difficult decision they faced. But now there is no avoiding the magnitude of the situation. What is being discussed here today affects not only Russia and NATO members, but the entire planet.

The White House, Washington, DC

27 March 2028, 12:15 UTC

While NATO representatives convene in Brussels, 6,000 kilometres away a fifty-four-year-old top Russian diplomat enters the West Wing of the White House. He is on his way to meet the US president's national security advisor. His task, as given to him directly by the head of the Russian presidential administration, is to convey the message that Russia does not want war with NATO but is prepared to wage it, and that Russia has no ambitions beyond controlling the city of Narva and making it part of its territory.

The national security advisor waits for the slim but well-toned man in his office. He too knows that the outcome of this conversation could determine how the president responds to Russia's aggression.

'Welcome. Wonderful to see you,' he says, greeting the Russian diplomat with almost too much exuberance, and points to the two-seater sofa in the middle of his office. 'Please, take a seat.' He himself sinks into a single armchair opposite. 'What can I offer you? Coffee? Tea? Or something else?'

'A tea, perhaps,' replies the diplomat, quickly adding, 'with a dash of milk.'

Once the tea has been served, the national security advisor begins the official part of the conversation. 'What brings you here?'

'Nothing less than the survival of human civilization,' the diplomat declares with a touch of melodrama.

The national security advisor takes a deep breath, exasperated. He knows that this conversation is intended to convey an important message to the American president, but this laboured opening gambit from his counterpart is irritating, all the same.

'And how can this be guaranteed?' he asks with feigned naivety.

'Look,' says the diplomat, sensing his opening words were a little overdone and adopting a more austere tone. 'My country has a history, a great history, and in the last thirty-five years we have had to endure being deprived of our core territory. We have had to endure humiliation, and our compatriots outside Russia are increasingly subjected to repression.'

After a short pause, during which he takes a sip of tea, he continues. 'Those times are over. We will protect our people if others do not. And we will protect them at any cost.'

'At *any* cost, Mr Ambassador?' the national security advisor challenges him.

'Yes, you understood me correctly. At any cost.'

A deliberately meaningful pause follows. The diplomat looks the national security advisor straight in the eye. 'Rest assured, we have not only the will, but also the means to do so. And why, some in my country ask, do you, the great American nation, refuse to understand this? Why do you keep doubting my country's resolve?'

'No one doubts your country's resolve, but don't we all have the same standards, the same rights and the same obligations?' asks the American, trying to steer the discussion in a more pragmatic direction.

The Russian leans back on the settee and crosses one leg over the other. It's clear that he has been waiting for this question.

'You – not you personally, but your nation – have achieved your great stature only by constantly flouting the rules and failing to fulfil your obligations,' he says. 'From America's perspective, rules seem to apply only to others, and only others have obligations. That era is over and we're not going back. Today, it is no longer the United States and its European vassals who dictate to everyone else what they should and shouldn't do.'

The national security advisor knows he has to move the conversation on. But how?

'Let's get into specifics,' he begins. 'We have a serious challenge facing our two countries right now.

Russia has violated the territorial integrity of one of our allies, and we are faced with the question of how to respond.'

'We have not violated anyone's territorial integrity; we are merely protecting our compatriots living abroad from persecution and oppression. Nothing more.' Moscow's emissary speaks in a tone that's unusually strident for a diplomat. 'And as you know,' he continues, 'the independence of the Baltic states is an artificial construct. Historically, they belong to Russia. But we are not questioning the right of these states to exist; we are solely concerned with protecting our people.'

'We could solve the problem, then, by asking our partner Estonia to meet your demands regarding the Russian minority,' suggests the national security advisor, nudging the conversation towards a possible solution.

'I'm afraid it's too late for that now. With the very best intentions, we have been drawing attention to the difficulties faced by our compatriots for long enough now, and there has been no change. We do not trust the Estonian government to protect the rights of Russians. That is why we have felt compelled to take matters into our own hands.'

The American sees that it's time to speak plainly with the ambassador. Clearly, there is no possibility of discussing a diplomatic solution at the moment.

'But you are aware that we cannot leave this provocation unanswered. Not only is our credibility at stake, but it cannot be ruled out that your example will be followed – and if that happens, what kind of world would we be living in?'

'Indeed,' replies the diplomat with a sardonic smile. 'We are of course aware of the military might of the United States, which has achieved such outstanding successes in Iraq, Afghanistan and also in Ukraine over the last decade. But rest assured, my country is prepared to do everything in its power to protect our Russian citizens in Estonia. And you must surely be aware that we have the necessary capabilities on land, at sea, in the air, as well as in space and in cyberspace. Furthermore, I wonder – and I hope you will allow me to be so candid – whether the Americans would be prepared to accept unfathomable damage on their own territory for the liberation of what is, from an American perspective, a small town in Eastern Europe?'

There it is, on the table: the threat of nuclear weapons. Apparently, Russia really is prepared to risk everything to achieve its goals. Or they are bluffing. But NATO will only find out if it is just a bluff by testing the Russian threat. And if it isn't a bluff, then the test could lead to the greatest catastrophe imaginable.

'I believe I understand you very well,' says the American slowly and emphatically. 'Without speaking for my president, I would like to ask you to convey to yours that the United States has no interest in a confrontation of this magnitude, but at the same time we cannot simply accept such a flagrant violation of international law. You must understand that we shall have to consult internally and with our allies on what an appropriate response might be.'

'Of course, I understand entirely,' replies the diplomat. 'And I think I speak on behalf of my government when I express the hope that the response you find will be one that is in the interests of peaceful coexistence between all our peoples.'

With these words, the diplomat stands up, approaches the national security advisor with an outstretched hand and, after the obligatory handshake, leaves the office with a determined and steady gait.

No sooner has he disappeared than the national security advisor calls in his most trusted colleagues and instructs them to convey Russia's message to the key NATO states via their various channels: in the worst-case scenario, they are prepared to do anything.

80° 49′ 35.2″ N, 66° 27′ 12.5″ W

28 March 2028, 10:27 UTC

'Prepare to surface.' The captain gives the order and the crew repeats it to make sure it's heard throughout the submarine. After the first officer and the engineer have checked the systems, they report back that the vessel is ready. The 170-metre-long metal tube rises slowly to ensure the almost 110-strong crew come to the surface safely. Meanwhile, periscopes and sonar are used to check the surface of the water for obstacles, ships or other hazards. This is not only to avoid a collision, but also to check if the Borei-class submarine has been spotted and if enemy ships are already waiting on the surface. But there's nothing. The captain has managed to stay undetected by sonar all the way to Hans Island, the destination of the operation.

Although its approach has gone unnoticed, everything now has to happen very quickly. As the nuclear-powered submarine approaches the surface, the US early warning system in Greenland sounds the alarm, initiating countermeasures. After all, it is not every day that a submarine armed with up to sixteen Bulava intercontinental ballistic missiles appears off the coast of a NATO member state. The fact that each of these missiles has a range of over 8,000 kilometres and can carry between six and ten nuclear warheads with an explosive yield of 100–150 kilotons sets off alarm bells. But that is precisely the aim of this operation.

Already close to the surface, three members of the GRU special forces, the Spetsnaz, have entered the airlock, which fills with water after being sealed behind them. Once the pressure has been equalized, the outer hatch opens and the three frogmen leave the submarine. They don't have far to swim. Once they reach Hans Island, two survey the territory and stand guard, while the third places a bottle of Stolichnaya and a can of caviar pretty much in the middle of the 1.3-square-kilometre 'rock' and hoists the Russian flag. They leave as swiftly as they arrived. And before any NATO forces have even set out to respond, the boat sinks back into the depths of the Nares Strait, heading homewards at a depth of 400 metres once it's out in the Arctic Ocean.

Russia has pulled off its coup. The vodka and tin of caviar are a droll allusion to the decades-long Canadian-Danish dispute over this island, where the two parties would take it in turns to arrive, hoist their flag and leave behind a bottle of their country's national liquor. Hence the conflict being known as the 'Whisky War'.

Far more significant, however, is the fact that a Russian nuclear submarine managed to advance through the Arctic Ocean to Hans Island without being detected. A warning that they could now surface at any time, anywhere.

NATO Headquarters, Brussels

28 March 2028, 14:00 UTC

It's normal for there to be a strong international media presence when the NATO heads of state and government meet for their annual summits. After all, it's a consultation of the world's most powerful military alliance. But this Tuesday at the Brussels headquarters, the press turnout is a logistical challenge even for the highly experienced press officers. There are press accreditations from countries all around the world, and the requests for interviews, whether with NATO officials or with individual heads of state and government, are almost too much to manage.

The mood is tense. Ultimately, the question is whether, for the second time in its history, the alliance will invoke Article 5. But unlike after 9/11, invoking the collective defence clause this time would not simply mean NATO Airborne Warning and Control System aircraft setting off to monitor some airspace or other, but that the alliance and its members would be entering a war – namely a war against a nuclear power, Russia, a scenario that NATO has since its formation in 1949 been preparing for and simultaneously trying to avoid.

Unlike most other times, the outcome of this summit is not yet clear. The consultations between the countries' sherpas and national security advisors have not yet resulted in a consensus. Although there is agreement on the need to condemn Russia's aggression, no agreement has been reached on what the consequences should be. No one knows what will come of today's discussions in Room 1 of NATO headquarters.

Once the heads of state and government, flanked by bodyguards, have entered the meeting room and the doors are locked, it's time to get down to business. The room is filled to capacity. There are so many advisors present that many can't even sit in the second row.

The secretary general picks up the bell in front of him and rings it to signal that everyone should take their seats. When there's quiet, he takes the floor.

'Ladies and gentlemen, I welcome you to this special meeting of the North Atlantic Council at the highest level. This is a historic meeting. At the request of Estonia, we must discuss and decide whether the Council should declare a state of defence in view of Russia's aggression against one of our members.'

The secretary general looks around the room at the thirty-two heads of state and government seated at the long oval table, in alphabetical order according to their countries' names.

'I have had many discussions with all of you, in an attempt to reach a consensus. I have succeeded in this with regard to condemning Russia's aggression. We have found clear and decisive language for this in our final communiqué. However, differences of perspective remain when it comes to an appropriate response to the aggression. This is what we must discuss today. The world is watching us to see how we respond, and our discussion must result in a unified position we can present to the public. I would also like to add that the unity of our alliance should be our top priority in our deliberations. With this in mind, I open the floor.'

The US president is the first to speak. 'What we're dealing with here is a limited act of aggression by Russia, which we condemn. But we also appreciate the background to it. For years, Estonia has failed to respect or bolster the rights of its Russian-speaking minority. It's no excuse for Russia's behaviour, but it's a historical context you can't ignore. Ever since I took office, I've been calling for Europe to spend more on its defence. More. Much more. I keep saying: Europe has to pay its bills to us Americans. What's changed? Nothing. Rich Europe is still refusing to pay up and is still relying on our strength and our presence in Europe. But why should we always have to take the heat for Europe?

'War isn't the answer. And the way I see it, it's a limited action by Russia. Limited to Narva. I'm sure we can reach an agreement with Russia about withdrawing from Hiiumaa. What are they doing there? They're trying to intimidate us and threaten us, just like their nasty operation on Hans Island. But in a nutshell, and this is the message we've received from the Russians, it's about protecting their ethnic minorities. And that is an Estonian-Russian matter. We can help. And I'm prepared to help. We can do a lot to help. But I'm not prepared to lead my country into war. I am not prepared to risk World War III for Narva. That is my position. That's the American position. If you Europeans want to do something militarily, that's your business. But we won't consent to it or support it in any way.'

This vehement diatribe lands like a bombshell. Not only is the US president vetoing the invocation of Article 5, but he has also dashed any hopes of a compromise that might allow a purely European-led counter-measure against the Russian attack under Article 5. Without the United States, which still provides more than 65 per cent of NATO's capabilities, and without American reconnaissance and transport capabilities, Europe is hamstrung.

'Mr President,' begins the German chancellor, who is next to speak. 'I understand your frustration at the lack of European commitment. Nevertheless, I would ask you to consider that this is much more than merely a bilateral Estonian-Russian conflict. In my view – and I think I speak for many, if not the majority, of those present in this room – this is about the future of the European, if not the transatlantic, security architecture: a structure that, until recently, guaranteed peace, freedom and economic prosperity for all of us. The economic prosperity of the United States, I would venture to say quite frankly, depends on access to European markets. This access cannot, however, be guaranteed in the long term, if we bow to Russian imperialism. And how will you look in the eyes of the world? In China, Iran and North Korea, you'll be seen as weak, as someone who lacks the resolve to defend the freedom of the West, the freedom of the world. In the long term, such an attitude will cause considerable harm to your country.'

It is not often that a speech is met with an approving thump on the oval table, applause, or a murmur of agreement in Room 1. But now is one of those moments. Not only has the German chancellor precisely expressed the sentiments shared by some of his counterparts, but there is also hope that he has struck the right tone to persuade the US president to reconsider.

That's not the only response the German chancellor's intervention receives, however. In the comments following his tirade, it becomes clear that a number of states are leaning more towards the US stance. Besides Hungary, Slovenia and certain Southern European countries, Germany's closest European partner, France, is – under its far-right government – also turning its back on Germany.

'We have a responsibility,' the French president urges the assembled leaders, 'not to use our military power to destroy the foundations of our civilization. Russia has undoubtedly broken international law, but not to an extent that would justify using our full military might. We also have a responsibility for the security of our territory and our citizens, which we would violate by invoking Article 5 and the countermeasures it would entail. From France's point of view, there is therefore no justification for so irresponsibly risking the lives of our citizens.'

This means that two of the three most militarily powerful states in the alliance, which have the necessary nuclear means to act as a deterrent but also to escalate this conflict, are not prepared to launch a military response under Article 5.

It is with some bitterness in his voice that the NATO secretary general concludes, 'Ladies and gentlemen, I note that there is no unanimity on Estonia's request to invoke Article 5, and I therefore ask the Estonian prime minister to withdraw this request. If my request is accepted, I will close the meeting.' As there is no alternative, the Estonian delegation agrees to this proposal, and the meeting is formally closed.

The secretary general heads straight from the meeting room to the atrium of the headquarters, where the press conferences are held. His press spokeswoman announces him to the assembled international journalists, saying that he will make a statement but won't answer any questions.

He then steps in front of the many cameras and microphones and gives his brief statement. 'Ladies and gentlemen. The North Atlantic Council met today at the level of heads of state and government to discuss Estonia's request to invoke Article 5 in view of Russia's act of aggression against our alliance partner. While there was agreement among the participants of the meeting that the aggression constitutes a violation of the territory of an alliance member in breach of international law, the Council was unable to agree on the initiation of countermeasures. It was agreed that further talks would be held.'

After a short pause, he adds: 'I would like to make a personal comment. Today was a dark day for the alliance. Thank you.'

The secretary general turns away from the assembled press and, followed by his closest aides, walks to the far end of the atrium and takes the lift up to his office.

Rzhev, Russia

29 March 2028, 07:00 UTC

Sergei Rabotnik is a simple man. He works in a factory that produces agricultural machinery, is married, and has two adult daughters who have long since left home to lead their own lives. He's working the late shift this week, and this morning he's sitting in his kitchen as he often does, catching up on the news and drinking tea. He still has ample time before he has to get ready for work. His wife, Galina, a nurse at the nearby city hospital, is on the early shift this week. So he is home alone. He doesn't mind. At least he has some peace and quiet. As always, the small television is blaring away in the background and Sergei is busy poring over the newspaper – or rather the sports section, which is the only part he pays close attention to. For him and his wife, the newspaper and television are their gateway to the wider Russian world. When you live in a town with a population of 60,000, a few hours' drive north-west of Moscow, the capital seems a long way away.

Sergei is poring over the reports on the latest developments at his club, FC Tver, which is once again fighting to stay in the second division, when there's a sudden blast of music from the television. But not the Russian pop music or folk music you normally get. No, it's a fanfare.

Confused but curious, Sergei looks up from the newspaper and shuffles his chair around to face the television, which is on the fridge.

If they're playing a fanfare, it must be important, he tells himself. And indeed, it looks as if something major is happening. The state channel Rossiya 1, which is on a continuous loop in the Rabotniks' home, is broadcasting live from the Kremlin. It appears to be some kind of ceremony. The camera pans across those present: elegant men and women dressed in suits and gowns, but also uniformed soldiers with medals of honour and combat medals on their lapels. There must be a good 200 to 300 people gathered in this hall. Why? Sergei wonders. He hasn't seen anything in the paper or on television about something important happening today. He must have not noticed it, he thinks. That must be it. Politics isn't really his thing, after all.

The camera pans several times over the heads of the guests, then cuts to a different view. Next, the golden Kremlin doors with the two honour guards. A suggestion that this is a gathering hosted by President Obmanshchikov. Because it's only the most powerful people in the country who pass through these doors. The two young guards slowly open the huge, weighty doors, and the camera shows Obmanshchikov striding along the red carpet, followed by two men – one to his right, the other to his left.

The closer Obmanshchikov comes to the camera, the better the other two men can be seen. The one to his left is Vladimir Putin and the one to his right is the president of Belarus, Alexander Grigoryevich Lukashenko. Both are getting on a bit, and beside the young and dynamic Russian president, they look like ancient Soviet apparatchiks.

The camera follows the three men to the podium and then pans to the crowd, who are giving them a standing ovation. After what feels like an eternity of thunderous applause, the audience resume their seats and quiet descends abruptly in the hall.

Obmanshchikov steps up to the microphone to give his address. 'Friends,' he begins, and there is something special about his use of the word 'friends'. Normally he would greet those present as 'ladies and gentlemen', but he chooses 'friends' – a familiar, informal form of address. Unusual, thinks Sergei Rabotnik in his kitchen, taking another sip of tea.

'Friends,' Obmanshchikov repeats, 'today is a special day, a great day for our Motherland. Today is the day when the greatness of our country will be restored. Our country and our Russian civilization. For today,

I can declare that Narva has returned to the bosom of our great nation. But that is not all. Today is also a day of progress on the Russian-Belarusian Union Treaty with Alexander Grigoryevich Lukashenko. We have agreed that our two nations will become one by 1 June 2030. The close cooperation of recent years will be transformed into a joint union. One parliament, one army, one president. Russia will thus return to its former strength.

'Since 2014, we have fought against those forces that have sought to keep Russia small, that have wanted to prevent us from taking our rightful place in the world, and we have defeated them. The West, with its aggressive anti-Russian policy, its decadence and its perverse view of humanity, has been defeated, at great cost, which – as we can say today – has not been in vain. We have defeated the Ukrainian fascists, and we have defeated their supporters. I have agreed with the American president to hold talks on the reorganization of the European security architecture and on certain global issues, which will begin shortly.

'We have achieved all this on our own, battling the most lethal powers in the world, which have sought to humiliate and crush our great Motherland. But we also have friends who have always stood by us. My gratitude goes first and foremost to President Xi. But President Modi has also proven himself a loyal friend of the Russian nation in these difficult times for us.

'Together, we strive for a peaceful world where power is distributed across various poles. A world that is just and fair for all peoples. As advocates of the Global South, we want to contribute towards the good of all. There will no longer be a global politics where one power tells others what they may and may not do. Those times are over.

'None of this – and I would like to emphasize this point – none of this would have been possible had it not been for one man taking the fate of our country into his own hands almost thirty years ago, leading us from our darkest hours to our greatest heights. We owe this man, Vladimir Vladimirovich Putin, our eternal, deepest gratitude and—'

The rest of his sentence is drowned out by thunderous applause from the audience.

Sergei Rabotnik turns his chair back towards the table and leans over the newspaper. He has to be at work in three hours. So, still plenty of time, he thinks to himself.

Moscow and Beijing

30 March 2028: A new centre

It is late at night when President Obmanshchikov picks up the phone to call President Xi. The phone rings twice and then is answered in Beijing. 'Mr President, good to hear from you. How are you?'

'I couldn't be better,' replies Obmanshchikov. 'History is moving faster than it ever has in the last hundred years, Mr President.'

Obmanshchikov can't see the smile on the other man's face.

Xi feels like he's at the apex of his power. His plan, developed from that of his predecessors, seems to be working. The goal is in sight. The might of the US has been broken and Chinese domination of the world is within reach. There is satisfaction in President Xi's voice as he replies, 'Yes, and we will determine the path it takes.'

Afterword

As explained in the foreword, in academia, scenarios like this are based on the continuation of observable trends and developments. They're not plucked out of thin air and neither do they exist in a vacuum. Nor are they a representation of inevitable developments. On the contrary, we develop scenarios in this way precisely so that we can prepare for them and stop them from happening.

In this context, we should conclude by asking which factors in this scenario would lead to Russia winning. Why would NATO fail the test it is being put through? How realistic are the events described, and what can we do to prevent this outcome from becoming reality? What's key is the lessons we learn from this scenario for the confrontation with Russia. Because it will continue, regardless of how and when the conflict in Ukraine ends. Russia will remain the central security threat in Europe for the foreseeable future.

Nuclear coercion

Above all, we must mention the success of the use of the nuclear threat. Since the beginning of its full-scale invasion of Ukraine in 2022, countries providing military support to Ukraine have been on the receiving end of Russia's threats to use nuclear weapons. Sometimes these threats have been directed at Ukraine, sometimes at the supporting countries. But in all cases, these threats have not been without consequences. Although there has been no evidence that Russia has indeed prepared to deploy nuclear weapons – for example, by removing warheads from storage sites to transport them to launch systems – the mere threat of their possible use has had an impact.

First of all, in many countries it has boosted what might be described as fearmongering, or even trading in fear.* The group of 'fear merchants' is a diverse one. It includes people defending Moscow's corner out of ideological conviction, former military personnel trying to make up for their insignificance to the public, journalists who seem to feel at home on the extreme right or left of the political spectrum, and a small throng of researchers. And they're buoyed by a large number of social media users and trolls.

* The following paragraphs are taken from an op-ed I published in *Handelsblatt* on 6 December 2024 entitled 'Die Angstunternehmer' (The Fear Merchants).

This group has taken the general public's and some of the political elite's justified fear of a widespread escalation of the conflict and turned it into their business model. Even before the full-scale invasion, they argued that all of Moscow's demands should be met in order to prevent an attack. And since the beginning of the hot phase of the war, they have constantly reminded us of their concern that any arms deliveries will inevitably lead to escalation, and possibly even to the use of nuclear weapons. Russia is unbeatable, they argue, and Ukraine should surrender as quickly as possible. With their vocal presence in the media and on social networks, this group has managed to unsettle a significant portion of the population.

We are seeing the impact. Polls show a growing number of people are in favour of greater caution in the transfer of certain weapons systems and support the idea of a ceasefire on Russian terms. This segment is still not the majority, but the longer the war continues, the more it grows. Democratic politics can't ignore this; after all, this group represents a significant portion of the German electorate, and in eastern Germany the party system was convulsed by them in the last elections.

Politicians have responded by delaying and reducing military aid. The difficult military situation in which Ukraine finds itself at the time of writing is in part due to this hesitance. Of course, Ukraine has also made some glaring errors – and still struggles with recruiting new soldiers, for example. But it also took far too long for European countries even to supply Ukraine with a small number of modern battle tanks. Russia used this time to reorganize its troops and, above all, to build extensive defence works in southern Ukraine, which ultimately led to the failure of Ukraine's counter-offensive, launched in summer 2023.

However, the nuclear threat also led to restrictions being imposed on Ukraine regarding the use of the weapons systems supplied, effectively forcing the country to defend itself with one hand tied behind its back. In other words, Ukraine was expected to fight in a way that its allies would never do themselves.

All military aid to Ukraine has been provided under the fearmongering scenario of a possible nuclear escalation. It has always come too late in view of the military situation, and is always too little to enable the country to defend itself successfully against Russia. The lesson Russia draws from these experiences is that nuclear threats work to deter the other side from taking certain measures. And so, Russia's nuclear threats with regard to Narva, as hinted at in my scenario, and the resulting consequences for cohesion within NATO are not the stuff of fantasy, but a realistic conclusion that can be drawn from the events of the last few years. Of course, we can't simply pretend that there aren't any nuclear weapons. But one lesson to be learned from recent events is that we must be aware of the coercive psychological mechanisms associated with threatening the use of nuclear weapons, and factor into our own thinking the fact that Russia uses such threats deliberately and tactically.

Lack of strategy

Another factor that is key to any analysis of the situation in Ukraine, and which may continue to have an impact in the future, is the fact that there has never been a clear strategy among Western leaders. But there has long been a refusal to acknowledge that Russia's war of aggression is much more than just a war to destroy Ukraine. In essence, it is a conflict over the world order – over the future structure of the international system. The states that want to maintain the liberal world order are going head-to-head against those that want a radical overhaul of the system. Political leaders have been far too slow to grasp this, and there still isn't a sufficiently widespread understanding of this insight, which has left Western leaders underestimating the growing military cooperation between Iran, China, North Korea and Russia. As a result, far too little effort has been put into preventing this cooperation, and there has been a consistent failure to join the dots between various global conflict hotspots. Ultimately, this has contributed to the emergence of a kind of military bloc which, in my scenario, comes to Russia's aid through the use of diversionary tactics.

Furthermore, this lack of strategy among Western leaders has been evident in the corresponding lack of any clear definition of what their goal is in supporting Ukraine. Is the aim to help Ukraine be in a position to liberate its territory from Russian occupation? Is it to allow the Ukrainians to destroy Russia's military capability so that it no longer poses a threat to the rest of Europe? Is it to enable Ukraine to hold out until Russia agrees to a peace compromise? Or is the intention to pursue all of these goals simultaneously?

To this day, it remains unclear what strategic goal the countries supporting Ukraine are pursuing. What is clear, however, is that the phrase so often used by former German chancellor Olaf Scholz, 'Ukraine must not lose, Russia must not win,' is not in itself a strategy, because it leaves these questions unanswered and replaces workable operational goals with fuzzy notions. Without a clear strategy, however, there can be no clear course of action when it comes to support for Ukraine. The latter derives from the former.

As the conflict progressed, the fear of a disintegrating Russia as a result of Moscow's defeat in Ukraine began to outweigh the desire for a Ukrainian victory among many political leaders. The so-called Prigozhin mutiny of 23–24 June 2023, or 'Wagner Group rebellion', when the militia of the renegade mercenary leader was able to sweep through parts of Russia for twenty-four hours unchallenged and without any significant military resistance, advancing to within 70 kilometres of Moscow, fuelled fears in Washington – and I would add, in Berlin – of a civil war within Russia, a country with 6,000 nuclear warheads.

However, the lack of a clear drive towards a Russian defeat was also thanks to the pious wish of many parties that Moscow would eventually come to see that this war was not worth fighting. Some even seemed to believe that Putin was just waiting for a suitable offer from the West to come to the negotiating table and agree a peace treaty. Far too slowly, and far too late, did Western leaders start to appreciate that Putin has no interest whatsoever in a peace based on compromise. But to this day, hopes remain that the Russian president will see reason. The question mark over the Russian president's intentions – a recurring theme throughout the scenario in this book – is eminently plausible given the persistent misperception, since Putin first took office in 2000, that the Russian leader is ultimately as interested in diplomatic solutions as his democratic counterparts. For far too long, Putin was not seen for what he is: a dictator for whom the use of force is a legitimate means of implementing what he considers to be Russian interests. To an extent, some leaders still have their heads in the sand about this. This has to change if the West wants to survive a scenario such as the one described.

Fatigue

In this scenario, fatigue plays a key role, on both a social and a political level. Besides eliciting fear through the threat of a nuclear escalation, Putin's strategy has been to rely on fatigue in democratic societies. The simple logic underlying this strategy is this: the longer the war drags on, the greater the economic burden, and the more likely it is that electorates will waver in their support for Ukraine and that a mood will emerge within society that governments have to take into account in decision-making.

Putin therefore believes that a dictatorship can wage war for longer than a democratic society, and it would appear he is not entirely wrong in this assumption. The longer the war has dragged on, and the less substantial the Ukrainian successes, the more a growing section of the population in many countries has begun to doubt whether their support for Ukraine has been worth it. Support for sanctions on Russia has dwindled with a rising perception of the ensuing cost. In some countries, right-wing extremist and, in some cases, also left-wing populist parties have benefited from this fatigue, by making the cost of the war a central theme of their electoral campaigns. And since we've seen how the acceptance of Ukrainian refugees has been exploited for propaganda purposes – and not only by these parties – the societal rifts hinted at in the scenario seem more than plausible as the flow of refugees continues.

However, there's another aspect to societal fatigue. Despite warnings from almost every defence minister or chief of staff – and even from heads of state and government – that Russian imperialism will not rest at Ukraine, that Russia is already preparing militarily for the day after, and that a future military conflict between NATO and Russia cannot be ruled out, large swathes of the population remain sceptical about such predictions. You can't really blame them. After all, day in, day out, they're witnessing the heavy losses in life and equipment suffered by the Russian armed forces in their conquest of Ukrainian territory. This raises the question of how Russia would be able to mount another large-scale military operation in just a few years, especially against NATO.

These doubts are further reinforced by targeted disinformation campaigns, contributing to the fact that for many people this possible future is inconceivable. But if we can't conceive of it, it becomes difficult for political actors to prepare for such eventualities. There is then no broad social consensus upon which to make decisions about higher defence spending, accelerated armament processes, or the reintroduction of universal conscription in countries where it was suspended or abolished in the last thirty years. Indeed, it's up to politicians to exercise conscious political leadership on such questions, not to negotiate these issues merely with an eye on public opinion and upcoming elections. This leadership has been lacking, even when it is urgently needed. After all, this current conflict could lead to the Russian Federation preparing for a possible future war against NATO or a NATO member state, while the European NATO member states are lagging far behind.

The capability gaps mentioned in the scenario (air defence, deep strike capabilities) are real, not fictitious, as is the lack of capacity to expand. It is therefore not unrealistic that Russia would put NATO to the test, as portrayed. The Kremlin is well aware that the alliance lacks rapid response capabilities, that the alliance member states and their populations are wary of conflict with Russia, and that Article 5 of the North Atlantic Treaty does not imply an automatic obligation to provide assistance. Since Donald Trump took office, there has been considerable doubt as to whether the US would come to Europe's aid in an emergency. US defence secretary Pete Hegseth made it quite clear at the Ramstein group meeting of 12 February 2025 that the US no longer sees itself as Europe's primary guarantor for security. This could make it more tempting for Russia to carry out a NATO stress test. Without the availability of American 'strategic enablers' (strategic air transport, air refuelling capabilities, cruise missiles with a range of over 2,000 kilometres, and, above all, satellite reconnaissance), Europe may be able to defend itself but is not necessarily fit for offensive action.

At this point, it should be stated quite clearly: if the scenario developed here – that is, a geographically limited test of the resilience of Article 5 – were to lead to the outcome described, then Russia would have achieved its goal. Moscow would have finally destroyed the European security architecture as it has existed for Western Europe since 1949, and for Central and Eastern Europe and the Baltic states since 1990. If the member states no longer believe that Article 5, the collective pledge of mutual assistance, is valid, then NATO is finished, as it no longer fulfils its intrinsic purpose.

What can be done?

As mentioned previously, scenarios are not only used to present possible futures in order to prepare for them; they can also serve to prevent precisely those futures from coming to pass. It is important to influence the factors in the present that a scenario then projects into the future. We'll finish by considering what this means in the case of the scenario presented in these pages.

Donald Trump was inaugurated just as I was completing the first edition of this book. As was to be expected, his campaign promise to resolve the Ukraine-Russia war within twenty-four hours came to nothing. Even he realized fairly quickly that it was going to be some time before a ceasefire or a permanent settlement could be reached between the two countries.

My scenario is based on the assumption that the US will withdraw its support for Ukraine and then largely pull back from Europe in order to focus on Asia. This is a plausible direction, and the first weeks of Trump's second term made it even more likely. Being able to visualize the consequences helps us to understand the strategic situation the European NATO states find themselves in. When it comes to the existential question of its own security, if Europe is to become independent of decisions being made in Washington – decisions they can only influence to a limited extent – then now is the time to act.

But a US withdrawal is not inevitable, at least not immediately. Around the time of Trump's inauguration, his national security team seemed to have come to the conclusion that Russia could not simply be allowed to have its way in Ukraine. This would only embolden Russia in its neo-imperial ambitions and pose a permanent threat not only to the rest of Ukraine, but also to neighbouring states. Secondly, and we might assume more importantly from the perspective of Trump's confidants, the US president would appear weak in the eyes of Putin and Xi, something to avoid at all costs, not least to prevent other countries from pursuing a military approach to redrawing their borders.

That is why initially it seemed the new administration might conclude that it should continue to provide military support to Ukraine, so the Ukrainians might stabilize the front and enter any negotiations from the best possible starting point. Trump also faces the challenge of how to persuade Putin to agree to a ceasefire in the first place. From Putin's perspective, the war against Ukraine is going well at the moment. With the decline in arms shipments to Ukraine, Russian troops have gained ever more ground in Donbas, meaning Putin currently has little or no incentive to seriously engage in negotiations. I therefore considered it possible that the Trump administration would, at least initially, do exactly the opposite of what happens in my scenario: that he would ramp up support, if only in the short term, and pursue a strategy of 'escalating to de-escalate' in order to make Russia willing to compromise and force it to the negotiating table. This prognosis, which could be extrapolated from various statements made by the Trump administration's national security team, did not ultimately prove correct.

This shows one thing above all: the core of Trump's politics is its unpredictability. One day, the American president calls Zelensky a dictator, the next he thinks nothing of the kind and wants to strike a deal that would give the US control over valuable commodities. Shortly afterwards, he humiliates Zelensky in the Oval Office, churns out the Russian narrative, blames Zelensky for the lack of peace and ultimately throws the Ukrainian delegation out of the White House without a deal. He then suspends American arms shipments, and it becomes known that US intelligence agencies are no longer sharing information with Ukraine, all of which plays right into Putin's hands.

On the other hand, Trump offers the Russian president extensive cooperation, pledging to lift sanctions and reinstate Russia to the G7, while his defence secretary makes it clear that the Americans will not participate in any military enforcement of a possible ceasefire in Ukraine. In an extremely innovative negotiating tactic, the Trump administration then announces before talks have even begun what concessions they are planning to make to Russia, including blocking Ukraine's NATO membership. Just as people start wondering how a Russian agent in the White House would behave any differently from Trump, he threatens Putin with sanctions and tariffs if he doesn't stop the heavy bombardment of Ukraine. Just a few hours later, however, he rules out tougher sanctions against Russia's shadow fleet, raving about how the Russian president wants to end the war and is going to be more generous in the negotiations than he needs to be.

Looking at it pessimistically, Trump is either a Russian asset or simply confused and haphazard. If you try to put a positive spin on things, the American president is pursuing a madman strategy, like Richard Nixon in the Vietnam War. A slightly modified approach would be to reduce reliability to such an extent that no one (neither opponents nor allies and partners) can be sure what Trump will do next, so that everything focuses on him and his agenda and he ultimately gets his way. The aim would be to break up an entrenched structure through deliberately irrational behaviour. If that's the aim, though, this strategy is doomed to fail – or else it will lead to the war in Ukraine ending in Russia's favour, as described in the scenario. Because time is on Moscow's side. While Donald Trump needs success in negotiations with Putin because that's what he's promised, there is little incentive for Russia to rush into talks. Putin can wait until he gets what he wants, or he can break off negotiations and let his troops continue fighting. Trump has already given away all the trump cards he might have used to put pressure on Putin. And a well-versed KGB man like Putin won't be intimidated by Trump's erratic behaviour.

Now, at the beginning of October 2025, as I revise this afterword, it looks as if the Trump administration wants to withdraw from efforts to find a solution to the war, whatever that might look like. After almost nine months in which Trump has failed to obtain substantial concessions from the Russian side – on the contrary, Russian demands have remained unchanged at their maximum – the administration seems to be realizing that this war is now threatening to become Trump's war rather than Biden's war in the eyes of the US public.

To avoid the impression that he is now to be ranked among the American politicians who have failed to bring this war to an end, Trump is withdrawing. This withdrawal is manifested above all in his refusal to continue to act as a mediator between the two parties. The US administration is not working to normalize US-Russian relations, especially in the economic sphere, but is withdrawing from efforts to achieve a ceasefire in Ukraine.

Furthermore, to avoid the impression that Trump has failed to bring about a ceasefire, attempts are being made to blame the Europeans for this failure. Trump says he is prepared to impose tough sanctions on countries aligned with Russia, including 100 percent tariffs on China and India if they continue to purchase Russian oil. However, he has said he will do this only with European support, knowing full well that there are countries – including Hungary, Slovakia, and Turkey – that would never agree to these sanctions.

In summary, at the time of writing, the Trump administration is actively withdrawing from this war, which means that Ukraine's survival currently depends solely on whether European countries are willing to increase military and humanitarian aid to the attacked state. However, when one considers that right-wing populists won the last elections in Czechia, that France is in a position of extreme political and economic difficulty, and that Keir Starmer is under massive pressure in the United Kingdom, doubts arise.

No matter what twists and outlandish notions Trump surprises us with, in order to prevent a scenario like the one described in the book, Europeans will have to reach the position where they can deter Russia on their own, without the help of the US. The argument that's always trotted out – that the key difference between Ukraine and the Baltic states is their NATO membership and thus the protection promised by Article 5 of the North Atlantic Treaty – is only valid to a limited extent, as demonstrated in this scenario and the Trump administration's statements about the alliance's security being contingent on increased spending commitments.

And if we look back at the history of NATO since 1949, there has been a persistent fear among European NATO member states that the United States might not keep up its obligations under the collective defence clause. Certain member states repeatedly questioned whether the US would really risk the destruction of New York to liberate Hamburg. If such fears were prevalent at a time when the whole of Europe felt the threat of the Soviet Union and the Warsaw Pact, then today it's reasonable to wonder why not only the US, but also countries such as Portugal and Spain (to name just two examples), should risk the lives of their soldiers and civilians in the event of a very limited regional escalation. This is precisely the question Russia is asking itself, and if we want to avoid a test like the one that plays out in my scenario, then we should ensure that Moscow's answer to that question is in our favour. In other words, that the Kremlin calculates that the risk associated with such an action is greater than the potential gain.

Any hope that Russia will be too weak in the future to attack other states, or that Russia's imperial ambitions are limited to parts of Ukraine, is pie in the sky. Putin has never left any doubt that he is committed to restoring Russian status and destroying the European security architecture. From his perspective, his is a historic task, and his willingness to sacrifice Russian lives in Ukraine and allow his economy to suffer is eloquent testimony to the missionary zeal with which he pursues his goals.

Going forward, Europeans will need to plough on with the efforts they have made over the past few years to equip their armed forces, in terms of both materiel and personnel. Since the Americans can no longer be counted on to bolster Europe's deterrence capabilities, Europe will have to do much more in the future. Because it's only if there's the sense in Russia that we are truly able and willing to defend every 'square metre' of our territory that we reduce the likelihood that Russia will at some point put the NATO alliance to the test.

There have been many developments in European defence since the first edition of this book. There has been a growing realization that the US can no longer be relied upon as a security partner since the Munich Security Conference of February 2025 and the Zelensky-Vance-Trump scandal in the White House. Most European countries are conscious that Europe will have to look out for itself and needs to do everything it can, and as quickly as possible, to ensure it can defend itself. To this end, unimaginably vast sums (800 billion euros) were released at the EU summit on 6 March 2025, and extensive measures were agreed on to enable member states to invest more in their defence. Even in Germany, sums are being discussed that were considered unthinkable even after Russia's invasion in February 2022.

It is therefore quite possible that Europe will rise to the historic challenge it faces. But this is by no means certain. My scenario shows what threatens to happen if the momentum that has now been generated does not lead to effective action, if it begins to wane, or if the large sums of money are squandered or trickle away. The decisive factor is not the amount of money made available or even pledged. What matters is the military capabilities that ultimately emerge. And time is crucial here. Even if more funds are made available, it will still be several years before traditional armaments are in place on European military bases. And in the meantime, the lack of US protection boosts Russia's incentive to test NATO as described in this book. How and for what purpose the money is spent is therefore also crucial. A rapid build-up of concrete deterrence capabilities is more important than the number of tanks on equipment inventories.

In my scenario, what plays a central role besides declining armaments is, in many NATO states, the lack of a public willingness to consistently face down Russia. A society that is unaware that its way of life is threatened by hybrid warfare, and that does not realize that Russia is seeking to undermine trust in the problem-solving capabilities of democratic institutions and processes through a variety of propaganda measures and disinformation campaigns – with the aim of discrediting democracy as a form of government – will not develop the willingness to become resilient or resistant. Resilience is the key prerequisite for mastering the challenges that European countries will face in the coming years. Russia will only be deterred and kept at bay if European societies are prepared to pay the price. In the extreme case of defending the alliance, this price will be measured in human lives, but it is already being paid in economic and political costs.

Anyone who hopes to increase defence spending will have to make cuts in other areas or rein in investments elsewhere. This will also involve a reassessment of government priorities.

The lack of resilience in society has negative consequences beyond the financial impact. The armed forces cannot fulfil their mission for long without public support. It is resilience that enables the government to fulfil its mandate of guaranteeing external security. However, for a society to develop the willingness to become resilient, its government needs to communicate very clearly to them what is at stake. Democratic societies are threatened by hybrid warfare, and ultimately what is at stake is nothing less than the defence of the democratic form of government – or, to put it more dramatically: defending how we live and how we want to live.